Keeping Faith in the Team

WITHDRAWN

2 1 MAY 2023

Keeping Faith in the Team

The Football Chaplain's Story

Stuart Wood

Chaplain to Cambridge United FC

DARTON · LONGMAN + TODD

First published in 2011 by
Darton, Longman and Todd Ltd
1 Spencer Court
140 – 142 Wandsworth High Street
London SW18 4JJ

ISBN: 978-0-232-52754-3

A catalogue record for this book is available from the British Library

Typeset by Kerrypress Ltd, Luton Bedfordshire
Printed and bound in Great Britain by CPI Antony Rowe, Chippenham

Dedication

To my Soul mate and Best friend – Hayley,
I couldn't do any of this without you.
And to my boys – Kieran, Curtis, Jordan & Corban
I am so proud of each one of you.

I love you all.

Contents

Acknowledgements

Thanks to:

David, for giving me this opportunity and providing heaps of encouragement along the way; Kathy, for your patience in editing; and all at DLT for backing this project.

My wonderful church family at Barnwell Baptist Church – you are an amazing group of people. Thank you for making it such a pleasure to be your pastor.

All the players, staff, directors and fans at Cambridge United Football Club. This book is your story, and without you not a word would have been written. A special mention to Jez and Greg for supporting me throughout and reading the draft through.

Martin, for your support of this project from day one. Sorry it didn't work out at United – all the very best.

All my fellow chaplains at SCORE and CPW who have knowingly, and at times unknowingly, encouraged me and inspired me in developing as a chaplain. A special mention to Matt for reading this through, writing the foreword, and all your helpful comments and advice along the way.

My family: Hayley – such patience; boys, for your understanding; Mum and Dad, for a lifetime of support.

And finally, God, without whom I am nothing.

Foreword

'A chaplain, at a football club, really?' is perhaps the response of many on seeing the cover of this book. We are perhaps used to chaplains in hospitals, the armed services or other work places but not really in sport.

And yet for those within the football industry this is no surprise at all as there is an increasing awareness of the important, in some cases vital, role a chaplain can play in the modern football world. Indeed, over the last 20 years chaplaincy within football has spread like wildfire. There are currently more than a hundred chaplains working throughout all levels of football in the UK from the Premier League, through the Football League, Conference and beyond. These chaplains are volunteering their time behind the scenes offering pastoral and spiritual care to all at the Club.

I first got to know Stuart six years ago at our annual conference at the National Sports Centre Lilleshall when he had just been appointed chaplain at Cambridge. Since then I have been impressed with his commitment to chaplaincy and extensive involvement at the Club and thus it was a pleasure and a privilege when he asked me to write the foreword to *Keeping Faith in the Team*. Stuart's account of life at Cambridge United gives an insight into the ups and downs faced during a season in the Conference Premier. It also shows the breadth of the chaplain's role from supporting injured players to engaging with the local community, from announcing the teams before kick-off to the scattering of a fan's ashes. And of course there's the football side of things too as Stuart reflects on the results and performances of the team. Stuart's own faith is also apparent as you read, not in a heavy 'preachy' way but more as something that is living and active, which influences his life both at and away from the Club.

There are many football books on the market and a few, if not so many, on football chaplaincy. However, *Keeping Faith in the Team* is, I believe, unique in that it is a chaplain's diary on what has happened on a month by month basis. For that Stuart must be commended for the way he writes with sensitivity, humility and interest and provides a series of snapshots at regular points in the season. I would also applaud Cambridge United for endorsing and supporting the project and for obviously being so appreciative of their chaplain's role.

This book will provide both an encouragement and a challenge to those already involved in sports chaplaincy. To those who were unaware of its existence this will give an interesting insight into both football and the specific help and support that a chaplain can provide. So, if you like football or you are interested in how faith can provoke someone to go and make a difference in their local community then this book is for you. I'm interested in both so really enjoyed reading it and hope you do too.

Matt Baker
Chaplain to Charlton Athletic FC
Pastoral Support Director in English Football, SCORE

June 2010

'I can't wait!' is the cry of many a football fan halfway through June, having had a few weeks without a match to attend. For many of those I speak to, there seems to come a point when the novelty of not going to a game and having a Saturday afternoon to do something different wears a little thin, and the attraction of the new season is something they're irresistibly drawn towards.

The close season is a strange beast. For the majority of supporters, alongside the free Saturday afternoons, it also provides an opportunity to save your money and, if you haven't got kids in school, to go on holiday. Of course, there are those who end up feeling lost without the week-by-week structure of games to attend, league and form tables to study and highlights programmes to watch.

Some people, my wife included, quite enjoy this part of the year as they get their husbands, wives or children back. And they don't have to contend with variable mood swings on a Saturday evening depending on how the team performed or the result achieved that afternoon. Ironically, by the time they've got used to having the family around again, the next season begins to beckon.

The players have an opportunity to rest, relax and spend time with family and friends before the long season gets under way again. Unlike in most other jobs, they have to take all their holiday in one go – once pre-season starts there are no more holidays until the end of the season, and for the 2007/08 and 2008/09 seasons at Cambridge United that meant play-off finals and a much later finish to the season than for most.

In 1986, a new system was introduced, replacing the one of three teams being automatically promoted and three teams relegated that had been used since 1898. To increase the excitement (and the revenue) and to encourage more teams to feel that they had something to play for, the final place available for promotion is now decided between the four teams that finish just below the automatic promotion places. So in the Championship, for example, the teams that win and come second are automatically promoted to the Premiership; the next four teams play each other (the team in third place plays the team in sixth place, and the team in fourth place plays the team in fifth place) home and away in the play-off semi-finals. The winners of these games contest the play-off final, usually at Wembley; the winner goes into the Premiership and the loser stays in the Championship.

In the Conference this system was adopted in 2002. However, only two teams move up each season so it is only the team that wins that gains automatic promotion, and the next four teams play off. The play-off final is usually about three to four weeks after the regular season's fixture schedule has come to a close, which does extend the season considerably and curtail the close season at the same time. Players requiring surgery can therefore end up missing the start of pre-season with not very long to get back on their feet.

Having reached the Blue Square Bet Premier play-off finals at Wembley in 2007/08, Cambridge United lost to Exeter City 1–0 and Jimmy Quinn departed as the manager. He was replaced by Gary Brabin who, perhaps unexpectedly, led United to a second successive play-off final at Wembley, only to suffer the same fate as the previous year, this time losing 2–0 to Torquay United.

Heading into the 2009/10 season there was a sense of anticipation at the club, which was dashed about two weeks into pre-season when Gary Brabin was shown the door. There followed a bizarre series of events, which ended just before the season started with Martin Ling being unveiled as the new manager on a three-year contract, with a much reduced budget, and talk of a three-year plan to get the club on an even keel financially and back into the Football League. At the start of the season there was hope of a top ten finish, which is exactly what happened, but with the reduction in budget we also saw a number of players leave or be released in an attempt to reduce the wage bill.

The season had started badly, but the second half of the campaign saw us string a series of good results together, and the season ended with a quiet sense of satisfaction that the club had achieved what it had set out to do.

As chaplain, seeing players that you have got to know well leave the club is not easy. In the transfer window in January 2010 Chris Holroyd went to Brighton and Hove Albion, Anthony Tonkin headed to Oxford United and others went out on loan, and at the end of the season we saw the departure of between eight and ten more players. Martin Ling had made the decision that he would either release players or offer them contracts after the season had finished.

So it was that at the beginning of May, I found myself at the club, standing in the dressing room when the players were called in one by one to see Martin to find out if they had been offered a contract or not. It isn't one of the nicest aspects of chaplaincy, but to my mind it's an essential part of the role, as we are there not just when things are going well, but also when things are difficult.

Some were expecting the knock-back and had prepared themselves for it. Others weren't so prepared, and for them to discover that they no longer had a contract, and therefore no income, was a shock and not easy to handle. Other players that did receive a contract offer were a little unsure quite how to respond, as they didn't want to make things awkward for their former team-mates. The reality is that, in that moment, they were stripped of all the bravado of being a professional football player, and stood there as young men, some with families and mortgages, and without jobs. This was about feeling frustration, pain and rejection, just like any other human being. In some way, I hoped that my presence demonstrated in a tangible way that God is not simply interested when things are great, but is also concerned for us when things are difficult.

And so heading into the 2010/11 season there were changes – new faces and fresh expectation. The strategy for Year 2 in the three-year plan was to aim for the play-offs by the end of the season by building on the previous season, taking the momentum from the end of that into the new one and keeping things steady financially. With some of the young players coming through and the acquisitions made, the play-offs were once again felt to be well within our sights.

Although the domestic football season had finished, there was the small matter of a football tournament taking place in South Africa. The hype in England (as always) had been building rapidly – this was our best chance of winning the World Cup since ... 2006?

Disappointing is not a word that could be over-used with regard to how England performed. Following the battle cry of James Corden and his World Cup show, I was 'Backing the Beard', which got quite itchy for a couple of weeks, and from that perspective I was delighted to be able to lose it minutes after the final whistle in the Germany game!

However, as a footie fan, I was quite willing to express my opinions as to what went wrong, and like the many other thousands of fans, I couldn't work out why I wasn't the England manager – it would have been so simple to win the tournament and bring the World Cup home!

Thinking about the World Cup, while we may think of the professional players as living the life of Riley, the reality is that for those involved in the finals, pre-season will have begun before the end of the tournament. They may have been able to grab a couple of weeks' holiday, but that will be it until the end of the next season. Some would say that this is a small price to pay, but what about their families or their kids? The life of a professional footballer does have its perks, for sure, but it also has its challenges, especially for family and friends – something that perhaps should be remembered occasionally, especially when the press take such an interest in all matters relating to our top players.

While the players are taking a break, for other staff at the football club the close season carries no such luxury. It is the time when preparations for the new season have to take place – negotiations with potential new players and their agents, getting sponsorship and commercial deals in place, selling season tickets, renewing the stock in the club shop, ordering in the new kit for the new season, re-seeding the pitch, painting, sweeping and cleaning ... so much work takes place that often goes unnoticed and unappreciated, and it is a side of football that as chaplain I am privileged to see and observe.

In my role as chaplain, close season provides an opportunity to catch up with office and ground staff – key personnel without whom the club wouldn't be able to function as well as it does. These are some of the unsung heroes of the football club – those who don't get the credit or adulation of the supporters on match days, but often have to bear the brunt of their moans and complaints. The ground and office staff are the people that can get overlooked during the course of the season, yet they still have to juggle work pressures and other commitments.

For me the other aspect of the close season is that it provides space to think more productively about some of the other things I am involved with at the club, without the week-by-week demanding schedule of fixtures.

As we left behind the 2009/10 season and prepared for the 2010/11 season there was an increasing sense of anticipation around the club, borne out of the hard work of many and what can only be described as one of the most stable close seasons at Cambridge United for a while. There was no change of manager or chairman, no high turnover of players or backroom staff, and only minimal changes to office personnel. Going in to the new season, which was going to be my sixth, I felt pleased to say that I knew the vast majority of the key people and wouldn't have to spend so long explaining who I was and what I did. I couldn't wait for the season to get under way.

But how did it all start? How did I end up serving as the chaplain at Cambridge United? The story began on 16 October 1996 – it was then that the little I had heard about football chaplaincy and Cambridge United came together in my thoughts. I was sitting on a National Express coach returning from a day conference in London, 16 days after I had taken up my post in Cambridge as a church youth worker.

I was born and raised in Bury St Edmunds, Suffolk – that's right, I am a tractor boy! I was blessed with my local team also being a successful one – the first game I watched at Portman Road was Ipswich Town v Liverpool with Ipswich winning 1–0, this in the days when Liverpool's team included Clemence, Neal, Thompson, Case, Keegan and Toshack, to name but a few … not a bad introduction to professional football!

Over the next few years I attended half a dozen games each season and developed my love of football, enjoying the successful Bobby Robson era – Ipswich were FA Cup winners in 1978 and UEFA Cup winners in 1981. One of the highlights of this period was the 6–0 drubbing of Manchester United, even with Ipswich missing three penalties (actually two – but the first was missed and then retaken and the retake was also missed!). Those were good days.

But as footie fans around the country will know, things haven't stayed that successful, and since the mid-eighties Ipswich have fluctuated between what is now the Championship and the Premiership – more often the former. But I have never felt the need to change my allegiance, unlike many today.

It wasn't just as a spectator that I enjoyed the beautiful game. I really enjoyed playing – in the back garden, for my school, for my church youth group, and then when I left school, in the Saturday afternoon Bury and District League. My love of the game is both as a supporter and as a participant (although nowadays more often the former than the latter!).

But alongside my love of football, there was also another passion that was developing in me. I was brought up in the Church, my family being very involved in the life of our local church, and at a young age I made a decision to become a Christian. For me that meant that I asked God to forgive me for the things I had done wrong and to help me accept this forgiveness; it meant choosing to live by God's standards and not my own – to have him as the boss of my life, not in a dictatorial way, but as a loving Father who wanted the very best for me. And at that young age, knowing that I would go to heaven when I died was a big thing for me.

Deciding I was serious about God was without doubt the most important decision I have ever and will ever make, as it is for anybody. Having made a decision at a young age, I found myself on a Christian holiday at the age of 12 and there I again decided that, yes, I was serious about God and I really did want to live by his standards and not mine. It didn't mean that miraculously I became a perfect person – far from it, but it did mean I had a reference point in my life, I had a purpose to my life and I had a very real sense of God being with me through all the ups and downs. It was like having a really good friend that was always there to talk to, always looking out for me and who never, ever got bored with me or frustrated with me.

It wasn't easy at all choosing to be different from the majority of my peers, but I have found ever since that God has never let me down. For sure, there have been highs and lows, but life has certainly been so much more fulfilling living as a Christian. The Bible records Jesus saying he wants to give us life in all its fullness – the most abundant life. As the one who created life, he should know what the best is, and it has been true to say that life has had more purpose, direction, vitality and meaning as I have chosen to live God's way and not mine.

After leaving school, I worked and trained as an accountant for six years – it ran in the family, with my Dad and two of his brothers, my sister, my future brother-in-law and I all working for the same firm! In 1988, at the final football match of my first season playing in the local league, I noticed an attractive young girl (with a very short skirt and fantastically long legs, it must be said!) who turned out to be the daughter of one of our supporters. A couple of weeks later, Hayley and I started going out and we were married five years later.

I loved those years dating Hayley, working as an accountant, playing football on Saturdays and running a youth club at the church, but in 1992 I felt God was asking me to train to work full-time in the Church. It wasn't something that I went looking for, but it started out as a thought, and grew into this decision that dominated my life – it was something I just couldn't shake off, no matter how hard I tried. After marrying in 1993, Hayley and I headed off to Bournemouth where I trained for three years at Moorlands College before moving to Cambridge in 1996. I must say that, much as I loved those years of courtship, accountancy, church and football, I love even more the work I do now.

So that's how I came to be sitting on the National Express coach, and I remember what I can only describe as God inspiring me to write down on a notepad – 'chaplain – Cambridge United'. I still have the notebook to this day. I didn't know what that meant – whether it was for me, or for someone else. I just sensed that it was a role that needed to be filled. It would be eight years before I would do anything further with this and nine years before it became a reality.

In 2003, St Andrew's Street Baptist Church, where I was now associate minister, began a conversation with Barnwell Baptist Church about the possibility of me working part-time with them, as they had no minister of their own and were not in a position to afford to employ one, being a small congregation of older folk meeting on Sundays. I began a dual role in September 2004 – still the associate minister at St Andrew's Street, but now also the part-time minister at Barnwell. (A team of others from St Andrew's Street also came with me to help reinvigorate the church at Barnwell.)

I remember one day attending Golden Years, the over-sixties club that Barnwell ran, introducing myself to some of these folk and listening to their stories. I couldn't believe my ears! Here were ladies in their sixties and seventies talking passionately about Cambridge United Football Club – and referring to it as 'their' club! I began to find out more about the club's roots in that community. And the penny started to drop. If I wanted to serve this local community, the Abbey Ward community in Cambridge, the football club could well be a way to do so.

So I made contact with Rev. John Boyers, who was by this time the chaplain at Manchester United Football club. He had previously been chaplain at Watford and had been instrumental in developing the idea of sports chaplaincy. He tells the story in his book, *Beyond the Final Whistle*.

When John left Watford in 1991 to take up the position at Manchester United, he also established SCORE, a charity with the express purpose of developing sports chaplaincy, not just in football but across a range of sports (visit www.scorechaplaincy.org for more information about the charity and the sports it now covers).

I had met John a couple of times at various events, had listened to him talk about chaplaincy and had spoken of my desire to see chaplaincy established at Cambridge United. We had maintained a level of contact over the years, so when I approached him again it was to revive this, although by this time there was another staff member at SCORE – the new chaplain at Watford, a guy called Ray Dupere – and it was he who met with me and helped me through those weeks of exploring the way forward, as he was based in the office closest to Cambridge.

John and Ray suggested I see whether there were any Christians at the football club, and if there were, talk to them about how best to approach the club – each club is different, and sometimes it's best to go through the manager; in other clubs it may be through the chairman, the CEO or the club secretary.

I made contact with Graham Daniels, a friend from my previous years in Bury who I had reconnected with when moving to Cambridge. He used to play for Cambridge United, had been manager at Histon and Cambridge City (during which time we explored the possibility of me being chaplain to City), and knew folk in the game in and around Cambridge. He told me that the physio at United, Greg Reid, was a Christian and suggested I made contact.

It was at Barnwell Baptist Church's Golden Years Christmas Party, which was held in the Harris Suite at Cambridge United, that I first met Greg. While the older folk were dancing away to Buddy Holly, Greg and I sat at the other end of the room and spoke about chaplaincy and possible ways forward. We agreed to meet again after Christmas.

The next day, I had a phone call from Greg to say that he had bumped into the chairman and had spoken to him about chaplaincy – if I could get some information to him by the following Saturday, they would discuss it at the board meeting that day. The information was duly provided, but the board meeting had another major matter to discuss – the sacking of a manager!

The rest of that season was one of the blackest in United's history – they were relegated from the Football League, sold their ground, went into administration, and but for an eleventh-hour intervention by then Sports Minister Richard Caborn MP, the club would have folded.

Once the future of the club was secure one of the directors, Brian Attmore, contacted me. He had been very interested in the idea of chaplaincy, and wanted to discuss it further. He had agreed to look at this on behalf of the board. So we duly met, he spoke to a few folk around the club – interestingly enough, folk who knew me (the secretary of the Vice-Presidents Club and the lady who washed the kit was a member at Barnwell and the club doctor was the mum of one of the girls who had attended the youth group I ran) – and took a recommendation to the board to appoint me as the club's first ever chaplain.

So it was that I was introduced as the new chaplain at the start of the 2005/06 season – the club's first in the Conference Premier. At that time Rob Newman was the manager, Tony Spearing his assistant, and they had four players on contract. There had been a large turnover in staffing, the club was in transition, and it was a challenging and uncertain time for many at the club.

The last five seasons have been full of highs and lows, with many changes as the club has had to restructure to allow for different playing budgets and a new way of operating. It has taken time to adjust to a different economy, not being a league side and receiving the benefits that it brings, especially in regard to youth development. During these five seasons there have been four different managers and one caretaker manager, five chairmen and one acting chairman, three commercial managers, four club secretaries and three general managers, to name but a few of the changes that have happened on the non-playing side. On the playing side, easily over 200 players have passed through the dressing-room doors in that time as well.

The implications for me as chaplain have been twofold. Firstly, the people that I have liaised with over my role have frequently changed, and with each change I have needed to explain my role and work out how to operate. And secondly, I may only get one opportunity to meet some of the players; there often isn't time to build long-term relationships, so if I want to leave a positive impression it needs to be almost instant. An extreme example of this occurred at our second appearance at Wembley in the play-off final in 2008/09. On the Friday before the game, United's goalkeeper, Danny Potter, was injured in training. With no other keeper on the books, Adam Bartlett, who had been at Kidderminster Harriers, was brought in on loan. I met him for about 20 seconds as I shook his hand in the dressing room at Wembley, wishing him well, but haven't seen or spoken to him since!

The outlook for the 2010/11 season was more positive – that close season there had been less of a turnover of staff and, rather than having to define my role, I had been able to build on it and talk through how best I could serve the club. But what is a club chaplain and what do they do? While there is some consistency through the support of SCORE for chaplaincy, the day-to-day function varies from club to club and from chaplain to chaplain. I am hoping that through the course of this book, you will gain an insight into what my role entails and why I do what I do, although please don't assume this will be the case for every chaplain.

During close season this year, the greater stability of the club had provided me with the opportunity to meet with the manager, Martin Ling, and the director of football, Jez George, to talk about my role and its relationship to the playing staff, both for the first team and the youth team, and to chat about how I could best work with their plans for the coming season. For the first time since I'd been in this role at the club, this season would see both squads training at the same facility, which would mean I could see all the lads at the same session. In the past few seasons, the squads had trained in different places, requiring a car journey between the training grounds, and these facilities, certainly for the first team, had been prone to change from week to week and day to day.

When I first began, it was the norm for the players to meet at the club, get changed and then head off in the minibus to the training ground. They would return to the club, get showered and have lunch. This proved a good time to sit down and chat, but the lunches stopped a few seasons back, which made it harder to find the time to be around the players. While I would go and watch them train, standing on the sidelines in all weathers, they were focused on their training, and while my presence was acknowledged, there weren't the opportunities to talk.

The prospect of having both squads at the same training facility, and lunch being an integral part of the programme, would mean more opportunities to be among the lads. Both Martin and Jez have been extremely supportive and can see the benefit of having a chaplain available.

As a result of these conversations, and through talking with the club secretary, Lisa Baldwin, we agreed that I would write a letter to introduce myself to the new players and to remind the returning players that I was available. Above all, it provided an opportunity for them to have my contact details without it looking awkward. I also wrote a letter to the parents of the scholars letting them know of my role at the club. We didn't know how much would come out of this, but at least drafting the letters helped me to set out simply and concisely what I saw my role as, and this had been agreed by Martin, Jez and Lisa, which was fantastic and a step forward in the work.

Although I am the official club chaplain, I have found other opportunities presenting themselves for me to be involved in the club –
particularly on match days. While I quite enjoy being able to sit and
watch the game, I have found myself with other responsibilities.

After I was established as the chaplain, there were occasions
when there would be a minute's silence before kick-off, and on
these occasions I was asked to introduce them as the chaplain and to
do so from pitchside. This was something that I didn't look or ask
for but it demonstrated that people at the club were thinking about
the role.

Then one match, the person who used to introduce the teams and
do the pre-match announcements from pitchside was away, and as I
had 'experience' of using the microphone I was asked if I would
stand in for him by introducing the teams, making a few announcements, and doing the draws and presentations at half-time. This I
agreed to, and so this season would be the fourth that I had been
involved with pitchside announcements.

This has led to some very surreal moments: two opportunities to
stand on the turf at Wembley Stadium and introduce the United
team ahead of their play-off finals; trying to read out the names of
the players in the middle of a snow storm; and 'commentating' on a
penalty shoot out with Timmy Mallett and two giant fluffy testicles
to raise awareness of testicular cancer!

There have also been some wonderful moments. I can remember
two seasons ago introducing Jez George and Matt Walker before
one home game. They had done a sponsored walk from Torquay to
Cambridge United, raising awareness of the fact that as a non-
league side our youth development gets no funding or protection
from the Football League – funding isn't dependent on how good
your scheme is but on what league you play in. As they did a lap of
the ground, between 3,000 and 3,500 fans gave them a standing
ovation. It was one of those moments when the hairs on the back of
my neck stood on end – it was very special.

Last season I was asked to offer some support to Martin Jordan, a
volunteer who coordinates the club's Smile Scheme. This scheme,
supported for the past two seasons by the supporters' trust, Cambridge Fans United (CFU), acknowledges the work of individuals

and charities in the community or people that are deserving of recognition in some way, and invites them to attend a game as our guests, providing 12 tickets for each home league game. Alongside this, we started to introduce the idea of bucket collections at home games, a different charity being invited to collect at the turnstiles.

My role within this scheme was really to get alongside Martin and support him in the work, and this seemed to work well; we managed to get a slightly higher profile for the scheme, with notes and photos in the match day programme, and I would make announcements about the scheme from pitchside.

During the close season, there had been many conversations about these two roles – how to develop and improve things, and how to make the match-day experience that much better for all who attend. Over the course of the season, this became an important part of my work, and the club looked to me to help them with their links to the local community.

So while players and many fans are enjoying a break, the work at a football club continues in earnest. It is a time for more strategic thinking without the demand of games, and it enables the work to be evaluated. Next season, spare a thought for those working hard to make the new season an even better experience for the supporters.

The close season was coming to an end – we were now gearing up for pre-season. As our thoughts turned towards the new season and prepared for the arrival back of the players for pre-season, I wondered what this new season would hold in store for the U's. I was excited about the opportunity to continue to be involved at the club – I love the opportunity to bring together two of my great passions, football and God – and I was eager to meet the new players and to catch up with the players returning. Bring it on, I thought!

July 2010

What does a chaplain do? I began the month supervising a work experience student, a lad from our church whom I had managed to set a placement up for. I found myself wondering how many other chaplains have had this privilege. I arranged a couple of days' painting, a couple of days in the office and some time with the youth team scholars and the first team. And then before I knew it, in his second week I discovered the club had arranged a placement from another school – so I then had two students!

My wife, Hayley, and in fact most others who know me, will testify that I find it too hard to say 'no', and as a result end up in all sorts of interesting situations. My take on this is that if I'm proving trustworthy in the small things, and in going the extra mile, I hope that people will remember that the chaplain was helpful – it wasn't simply about his agenda.

This has been crucial for me, and has become a foundational principle in my work at the club. From day one I wanted my role to add value to the work of the football club. I have never wanted the role of the chaplain to be viewed or understood as a role that took resources from the club – I just hoped that, in small ways, the chaplain would be known as someone who would offer help.

Perhaps it is just me, but I get so frustrated with how Christians and the Church are perceived, and perhaps rightly so. It seems to me that as Jesus walked on this earth he took opportunities to simply help when he could and to get involved in people's lives. When he turned water into wine (something I've been asked many times if I can do!!) he didn't do it so the people would come to church, or to build his own reputation, although this happened naturally as a result. No, he was at the party, the need at the time was for more wine, and Jesus was able to sort that situation out. There was no great speech, no great announcement – he simply served the people in the situation they were in and this had a big impact upon them.

So that is how I seek to live – if I can help someone, then I will. It isn't about me and my reputation; it's not that I want credit for being like that. To me, a Christian should model themselves on Jesus, and as that is how he lived, this is how I should live. I hope that it blesses those I work with and serve. I know that one of the dangers is that I can become a doormat, but I guess that is a risk I take. There have been many occasions when I have been taken for a ride, but there have also been many occasions when wonderful opportunities have emerged.

One of the things that I have come to realise more and more over the past season is that people's previous experiences of chaplaincy can either help or hinder opportunities in the future. I have benefited greatly from Martin Ling's very positive experience of chaplaincy at Leyton Orient with Rev. Alan Comfort. Reflecting on this leaves me keener than ever to make every moment count and take every opportunity to leave a positive impression of chaplaincy.

Pre-season therefore always carries a sense of anticipation and also a slight anxiety as I meet the new players for the first time – what is their previous experience of chaplaincy, or come to that the Church? Will I be welcomed or given the cold shoulder?

A challenge that has faced many a Cambridge United manager over recent seasons is the fact that they do not have their own training facilities. As I mentioned last month, the practice had been for the players to arrive at the Abbey Stadium, where they would get changed and then head off in the club minibuses to whatever training facilities they could find available that day – usually one of the University College sports grounds. At the end of training they would return to the ground for a shower and then off home. But this process could take away valuable training time travelling back and forth across Cambridge (which, to be fair, isn't a particularly nice place to have to drive around).

For those who don't know much about Cambridge University (and I don't claim to be an expert), the University is made up of a number of colleges, most of which have their own sports grounds (or at least share). These are immaculately kept, many with their own groundsmen who live on site. They are lush, well-established and provide very pleasant surroundings to train.

For the 2010/11 season things would be different. Cambridge United Youth Development – which includes the 16–18-year-olds, those known as the scholars, and hoping to earn professional football contracts, had for the last few years been developing a close working relationship with the staff at Clare College sports ground, and towards the end of the last season and over the close season, an arrangement had been made for both the first team squad and the scholars to train at the ground from October once the cricket season had finished. Until then, the first team would be training at the Pembroke College grounds.

So it was that one Friday morning I apprehensively made my way down to Clare College training ground on an overcast morning to be introduced to the scholars – the new first years arriving at 16 having just completed their GCSEs, and those returning for their second year. I expected to be greeted by Jez George, CUFC's director of football and the head of youth development. But he was delayed elsewhere so the coach Nolan Keeley met me.

The scholars train most days, and they also study for a National Diploma in Sports Studies. They also have the option of studying for an additional A level at Cambridge Regional College (CRC). They play as CRC in the Ridgeons League Premier Division; the only time they turn out as Cambridge United Youth Team is in the FA Youth Cup.

In the previous season I hadn't had much opportunity to be around the scholars, purely down to my own time commitments, and although I had got to know one or two of the lads – mainly those who had been injured – I was frustrated with myself that I was still stumbling over names.

When I arrived at the training ground there was a wonderful and bizarre moment when the lads were brought together and Nolan introduced me as the club chaplain and then handed over to me to introduce myself and explain what I did. Standing there in that moment, attempting to concisely sum up the role of the chaplain, I wondered whether, if I were in their shoes, I'd have wanted to listen to this. I doubt it, to be honest – I'd have wanted to be out there training! So I concluded, knowing that there was a letter for them that perhaps better explained my role. I stayed to watch them train for a while, testing myself in an attempt to remember the names of the second years.

Having spoken to Jez, and knowing the two squads would be training at the same facilities for the first time, certainly in my time as chaplain, had given me some confidence that this year would be better for me with regard to the youth team. Hopefully, the plan of being around much more would make a difference, and would leave the door open if anyone wished to make contact with me.

It is very noticeable that with at least a third of the first team squad having come through the youth team ranks at the club, the relationship I now had with these players was very different from what I had known in the past – they were very accepting of my role and of my presence around the club. It was also good to have watched them develop from their first days as first year scholars into professional footballers; both the way their game had developed, and the way they had matured and conducted themselves off the field was testimony to the work of Jez and Nolan.

Having introduced myself, and Nolan again reiterating how my role complemented the work he and Jez did, the lads shook hands and got back to the serious stuff of training. Interestingly, the difference with the second years was noticeable – they were much more willing to give eye contact, to give a little bit more than a 'hi' and to engage in even the most superficial conversations.

But as I reminded myself, the first years had just finished GCSEs, many of them had just left home for the first time, and they were only 16. I'd probably have been exactly the same! There would be more opportunity later on to catch up with them, to chat informally and to find out a little more about them and their backgrounds – both footballing and personal.

The following Monday, I was back at the club to meet the first team squad, as arranged with the manager. The lads were all in the dressing room getting their kit sorted out. I introduced myself to Adam Miller and Daryl Clare – two of the new faces – who were chatting. A few of the lads signed at the end of the previous season I had already met at a function at the club – James Jennings, who had arrived from Kettering, Danny Naisbitt and Danny Wright, who I knew from Histon. Conal Platt was the only other new face I hadn't met, and it was nice for a change to be able to welcome back quite a number of the lads who had finished the previous season. Alongside getting their kit sorted, they were being put through a gym session before a run and then some gentle ball work on the local common – a far cry from the nice surroundings of the college sports fields.

It was great to be back, to be honest, and to meet the lads again. Martin introduced me between drills on the common, with a bit of humour and banter that cannot be printed! But I've long come to accept that this is the world of football, and it doesn't faze me.

A few days later, watching them train at Pembroke College, there was still plenty of banter. Arriving early and in glorious sunshine, I found the lads still in the changing room, which provided a good opportunity to grab a few moments with some of the new lads – Adam Miller asked me if I was like the pastor in *EastEnders*, who in the storyline at the time was holding someone hostage in his basement! The training itself, once under way, was now a little more serious – the work rate had gone up noticeably, but there was still some good banter and a good atmosphere among the lads.

Each time I go to training, alongside the general 'hello' and 'how are you?', there are opportunities to chat to one or two more players in a little more depth, and the relationships become a little more natural. There is still of course a distinction – I am not one of them, and don't wish to be. The role of the chaplain is to be independent, so that if a player wants to speak to you, he can do so without thinking that what he says is immediately going to go back to the management, and likewise the management can speak to me without thinking I am going to pass this back to the players.

From the outset I have insisted that my role isn't simply to be the chaplain to the players, but rather to the club – and that includes the management, players, staff, directors and supporters. In bigger clubs I expect it becomes much harder to serve in this way, and I greatly appreciate the opportunities I have at Cambridge, which may well be peculiar to this context.

What do I do when watching them train? Ray Dupere describes chaplaincy as a 'ministry of presence' – it is about being around the lads as they train, watching and listening. The majority of the time I spend collecting balls, as when training on more open spaces, balls end up scattered around. This season, Martin had brought in a first team coach, John Schofield, to join him and player/assistant manager Paul Carden, and this had meant that Martin was able to stand back and watch rather than being so involved in the running of drills, for example. It also meant that I found times when I could stand and chat to him about what was happening and the atmosphere around the place, picking up things that might prove helpful. After drills and games, picking up cones, poles and so on all enable me to be around and not be in the way, and often again, opens up opportunity for some banter or a comment.

This season Martin had asked me to be around on Mondays as that was the day of the week that he felt best suits my work, and also what he had been used to at Leyton Orient. He suggested I brought my boots, as he was willing and keen for me to join in. The last time I'd trained with the first team, one of the players had ended up with a dislocated finger when his finger got caught in my jacket! I was a little excited about the prospect of being able to join in, although I realised my opportunity to be a professional player had come and gone long ago.

One Saturday in mid-July, I had arranged to take a couple of players along to a charity day – Adam Marriott and Jordan Patrick were the lucky ones. Through my work in the local school, I had got to know a lady called Suzanne and her daughter Ayesha. Ayesha was diagnosed with leukaemia when she was three and bravely fought this for four years. She then went into remission for five years. I got to know the family soon after she was diagnosed with a brain tumour at the age of 13. I had the immense privilege of visiting Ayesha and Suzanne, in hospital and at home, and when Ayesha finally lost her battle, of sharing in her thanksgiving service.

Suzanne had become involved in COPARS, a charity that had been established to support families of children and teenagers suffering from cancer. After Ayesha died, I was talking to Suzanne and discovered that obtaining funding was difficult, and that the work, which was greatly appreciated by the families and staff at Addenbrooke's Hospital's children's oncology ward, was under threat. I wanted to do what I could to help, so linking the charity up with Cambridge United was an obvious starter, and I made arrangements for the players to attend the charity's family day and in being there to demonstrate the support of the football club for this work.

It was in some ways difficult – there was no real structure to the day, and the children who the charity supports who are really keen football fans were too unwell to be there, sadly. But these two lads never moaned or complained, or looked for an excuse to leave early. Towards the end, the lads posed for a photograph with all the children present and it was great to see them interacting with these children and talking to some of the parents. The lads were a credit to the club and at the same time had to deal with the reality of children and young people whose lives were being cut short by cancer. The links between the club and this charity would be developed in the coming months as part of the club's Smile Scheme.

When I was appointed as the club chaplain, one of the reasons put forward for my involvement was to develop links with the community. This has become a remit that I have enjoyed and this would be enhanced in two ways at the start of the new season.

The Smile Scheme, which for the previous two seasons had been supported by the CFU supporters' trust, had now attracted a commercial sponsor, and I was invited, along with Martin Jordan, to attend a meeting with the commercial team and the sponsor to talk about how the scheme could develop and the plans we had for it.

This season we were hoping to dovetail our Smile Scheme tickets with our bucket collections in such a way that the club would have a nominated charity of the day. I would be responsible for ensuring there was an article in the match day programme, raising the profile pitchside, and working with Martin to ensure we had groups booked for each game.

It was very exciting to be part of this initiative – initially I got involved at the request of the club to offer some support to Martin Jordan, who had been largely left with this side of the club's activities, and they and he were keen to have some support. The meeting with the sponsors was well received and Martin and I were charged with the task of going ahead and booking in the various charities. The first charity to benefit was COPARS, following on from the charity day mentioned above.

During the close season I was also approached by David Matthew-Jones, the chairman of CFU, to see if we could meet, as the trust was keen to develop its community links and he wondered if I could help in this. Again, it was an honour to be asked and I hope that I will be able to help the trust and the club to be a more positive contributor to the local community, immediately around the club and also into the wider Cambridge community. This was another way in which my role was developing with regards to helping foster good links with the community. It would be fascinating to see where this took me and the club over the next season.

I've mentioned already that I have always insisted that my role isn't just focused on players and staff, but supporters as well. Over the years there have been a number of opportunities for me to share with families following the loss of a loved one. This has ranged from me taking the services of a loved one, to simply attending the service as a representative of the club. There are many supporters whose passion is Cambridge United – they may have been attending for years or they may have been stewards or volunteers, and I believe it is important that these folk are honoured appropriately.

There have been times when a minute's silence has taken place to remember the loss of a fan or player, and more recently there has been the introduction of a minute's applause. One of the more significant pitchside moments of last season was when I introduced a minute's applause to remember two young CUFC fans that had died tragically in separate incidents, and standing with their families as the crowd and players marked that moment will be one I will remember for a long time. Two weeks later I introduced a minute's silence as we observed Remembrance Day. These were two very different but equally poignant moments, both observed impeccably.

Towards the end of July, I was contacted by the club as they had heard of the passing of a CUFC fan – would I contact the family? Michael Wood had been a fan of the Us for many, many years. I phoned one of his daughters and was able to help with a number of queries the family had regarding their father and CUFC. After this, one thing led to another, and the family invited me to read a poem at his memorial service. As far as I know, I was the only club representative there, but the family were deeply appreciative of the fact that the club had marked this occasion.

These small acts, which cost little except time, can have a big impact upon families who are grieving. It is another way that I seek to serve the club and the CUFC community and hope that as people encounter the chaplain they are left with a positive experience of God and of the Christian community.

In connection with marking these significant and poignant moments, over recent years I have been exploring with the club the setting up of a Book of Remembrance – a number of clubs now have something similar. It is my observation, and that of many others, that following the Hillsborough disaster in 1989 and national out-pouring of grief following Princess Diana's death in 1997, there has been an increase in the use of memorials to mark the loss of loved ones – whether that be at the roadside or at another significant place, people are looking for somewhere to go to remember. And sports clubs can provide that space.

I have been hugely impressed with how Rev. Phil Mason, the Bolton Wanderers FC chaplain, has helped that club to mark these moments. At Bolton they had built into the outside wall of the new Reebok Stadium (so it is accessible 24/7) a window behind which is a Book of Remembrance. There is a page for each day, and each day the page is turned. Families and relatives can go there to have a few moments to reflect and remember, and there is a holder for them to leave flowers. Once a year, Phil holds a service of remembrance to which all the families of those whose names are contained in the book are invited, and at which all the names are read out. They have also established a walkway where bricks can be purchased – these can be used to mark a memorial or a celebration of another signifi-cant milestone in life. At this stage I am not looking to set some-thing like this up; with the possibility of CUFC relocating, maybe in the future we can also achieve something similar. But for now, we hoped to set up something simple but significant. The conversations with relevant parties at the club would continue and who knows what might happen in the course of the next season.

It was Bill Shankly who famously said, 'Football is not a matter of life and death … it is much more important than that.' Part of my role is to be there to help those whose experience brings death and football together, but more than that, to help the club to be effective and sensitive in its response to these significant moments too.

The pre-season games provide an opportunity for the players to test and improve their fitness, and to begin to gel as a team. At Cambridge United they usually try to get one or two teams from higher divisions to come to the Abbey. This pre-season we welcomed two teams from League One – Colchester United and Martin's former team Leyton Orient. The away games tend to be against some of the local sides. There may be arrangements with sponsors, clubs that scholars have come from, or personal links that lead to a number of local fixtures – this year Mildenhall, Lowestoft, St Ives and Cambridge City were among them. Some of these games are played with a more youthful side, some with the first team, depending on how the games fall in relation to one another and the training regime.

While these games provide a good opportunity for the players to have a run out at home, to test their fitness and to work on their team game, they also give the match day staff the chance to get a run out before the start of the season. The caterers can make sure everything is working, the stewards get back in the swing, the office staff get to grips again with match days and for myself, the team announcements and charity collections get the cobwebs blown off them and we can again look at how they are working ahead of the first home league game.

Leyton Orient was the only game I got to see in this period. It certainly was eventful from my perspective – I guess I managed to watch about 30 minutes of the 90! During the second half one of the Leyton Orient players, Jake Argent, had to be stretchered off and was taken to the medical room at the club. Whenever that happens, whether it is one of our players or a visiting player, I go to the medical room to see if there is anything I can do. Often with our own players there will be relatives or friends who I will be able to talk to and look after while they are waiting for news of what is happening. In the case of opposition players they are usually on their own and it can be a little bit lonely. There is one player who I still chat to when he plays at United who I spent a bit of time with after he got stretchered off a couple of seasons back.

At the Orient game, it just so happened that I had been chatting during the first half to their chaplain, Alan Comfort, and so I went to fetch him as the young lad was upset, fearing the worst. It is often in those moments of injury when players are at their most vulnerable. It has been these occasions over the years when I have had some of the most honest conversations with players. I can remember talking with one player, a tough centre forward who was afraid his career was over – his bravado was replaced with fearful vulnerability. I can remember another player beside himself at the thought that this was game over for him – sadly this proved to be true.

In the moments after a player is taken off, it can be difficult for them. Sometimes they are left alone – the physio has to go back to the touchline and can't do more until half time or full time; sometimes the club doctor will be involved, but again they will get the player to a place where they are stable, stitched and comfortable and then go back to the game. There have been many cases of players needing gashes stitched back together, and this is often not a very pleasant sight, especially for the family. So to be able to distract family members while the club doctor stitches is something I can do. Occasionally the player will just want to phone a parent or partner, and again I have been able to get a phone for them to use while they are lying waiting for the ambulance or for the physio or doctor to return.

Usually, I get some wisecrack about 'last rites' at those times, but nonetheless, it invariably is appreciated. I have found that my relationship with some players changes in that moment, and from then on there is a greater warmth as they realise that I'm not there to preach at them, just to be a friend.

Jake was only 17 years old and was making his first appearance for the first team – and it only lasted seven minutes. He sustained a serious injury to his knee, requiring cruciate ligament reconstruction. I was able to send a couple of messages via Alan Comfort and hoped to keep in touch to hear about his progress.

Over recent years I have taken on the responsibility of being the pitchside announcer, a role you will hear more about as the season goes on. The microphone I use is kept in the security room, and so part of my match-day routine is to return the microphone at the start of the second half once the half time announcements have taken place (we have another tannoy announcer who does substitutions, scorers, and so on).

During the Leyton Orient game, a situation had come to the attention of the stadium officer, Ian Darler, and the people involved were being monitored on the CCTV cameras. I recognised one of these individuals as someone I knew, and as a result I ended up offering to go and talk to this person. This eventually resulted in me being involved in helping the police with their investigation.

The game ended with a 3–0 win for Leyton Orient. From the little I saw, and what I was told, we seemed to have some difficulty in the last third – we didn't really create many clear-cut chances, but I was sure that as the players started to gel and get to know each other, things would gradually open up and the goals would come. So far the pre-season had been a little mixed – some good and some bad.

I am so thankful that Cambridge United has such a good club physio in Greg Reid. As you will remember, he was involved from the start, and not only has he been a fantastic advocate of chaplaincy, but he has become a very good friend. He and his wife are also members of the church at Barnwell, and it was a joy to baptise them both back in March 2009.

This relationship over the years has been a real highlight of the work. Greg is one of the few people at the club who have been in post for the whole of my time I've been associated with it as chaplain. We have often met to pray together at the club – not about winning or losing, but about important decisions, significant moments or injured players. It is my belief that prayer does work and I will unashamedly pray for folk at the club. In particular, I can remember many a time of prayer at the club in the six months between me contacting the club and my appointment, praying for Greg and the club during those difficult days. I also remember Greg and I meeting up with Ray Dupere of SCORE and spending a couple of hours talking and praying as we wandered around the ground.

If people ask me to pray for them, I will take them seriously and will see this as an honour and privilege. I believe in a God who longs for people to know that he really is there for them and really does want to make a difference in their lives, and answered prayer is one of the ways he uses to get their attention and to begin to think about him.

I have often been asked if I can put in a request for good weather, the right result in a fishing competition (one of Ian Darler's favourite requests) or the right balls to be drawn in the lottery! But there have also been times when I have been able to pray for a sick relative, a difficult situation at the club or at home, and as mentioned already, for someone who has been injured.

If I had a pound for every time someone made a comment about me praying for the result – either I have been, or I haven't been, depending on the score – I'd have a decent lump in the bank by now! It is one of the standard comments that gets bandied about among the supporters. But I don't mind that at all – I'll be more concerned when it stops.

Back to Greg, at the club the physio's room is my second home – it is where I naturally default to going. Partly this is because it is next to the dressing room – that is the domain of the players, and this is somewhere I can be without feeling that I'm getting in the way or am invading someone else's territory. It is here that I often get to chat to some of the lads waiting for treatment or being treated. Greg is also very good at involving me in the treatment – seeing him outside of the club situation he will let me know if there are players needing treatment, operations, and will let me have phone numbers if I need to contact players. He has been a real blessing. Alongside that, he is an extremely competent and very gifted physio, and does wonders with the players. It has been a privilege to have shared some of the dark times with him, and also to share in some of the highs.

As another pre-season got under way, it was an eventful month. There had already been one operation, Rory McAuley's knee surgery, a number of muscle strains and niggles, and Daryl Clare needing more intensive physio. Greg allows me to have access to the injured players and will encourage the opportunities for me to chat to them and get to know them. With Daryl it was a good opportunity to get to know him as he was new to the club, and while the rest of the lads were running about, to be able to stand and chat to him about his family and career while he was doing stretches and other exercises was really positive from my perspective, although his injury was hugely disappointing from Daryl's and the club's point of view as we wanted him out on the pitch scoring goals! But that's football.

I know that in other clubs the physio's room is an important place for the chaplain, but I am especially grateful to have a physio that is more than an employee of the club. I knew that as the season progresses the physio room would continue to be my base at the club.

August 2010

The build-up to the first game of the new season continued with another couple of pre-season friendlies – both away. First up was a Tuesday evening trip down the A14 to Bury Town, who won the Southern League Division One in 2009/10 and were preparing for their first campaign in the Ryman League Premier Division. Bury Town are the fourth oldest non-league club in the country, and are the home club of the Suffolk market town of Bury St Edmunds, where I was born and grew up.

So I took the opportunity to go 'home' for the evening and watch the U's. For me, travelling to the occasional away game is quite important. As described last month with the Leyton Orient game, with my match-day responsibilities and other things that crop up from time to time, I can sometimes miss large parts of the game. Travelling away frees me up to sit back and enjoy the game. It often also allows me the opportunity to chat to players not involved, directors or supporters, in a different way as I am not 'on duty'.

The other beauty about a club like Bury Town is that it is not segregated, so you are able to walk round and watch the game from different areas. So it was that I watched the first half standing pitchside with a couple of the directors, players' families and supporters. For the second half I sat in the stand with Conal Platt, Daryl Clare, Kevin Roberts and Rory McAuley – players not involved as they were injured. With three of these lads being newer to the club, it gave me an opportunity to talk to them about their previous clubs, and how they were settling at United as well as finding out a little about their families.

It was good to watch the U's play well – to see how the lads were getting on on the pitch and their team spirit. The new lads and young lads were joining in and performing well, with the second year scholar Jonathan Thorpe holding his own at right back, and Adam Marriott came off the bench to score a hat-trick.

Afterwards, I was able to sit in the bar with one of the club's directors and a couple of fans and enjoy a drink, chatting to the players and management as they came through for some food. For me it was a relaxed evening and I had enjoyed being able to watch a game without having to dash off to give half-time announcements!

With the fixture list out, I started to work out which league games I could travel to. I am fortunate to be able to travel on the team coach from time to time, and this is another opportunity to spend time with the players and management. The last time I travelled on the team coach was to the away game at Kidderminster on a Tuesday evening in March 2010, and on that occasion I was privileged to be able to sit pitchside in the dugout and watch the game from there. Although the result wasn't what we had hoped for (the U's losing 1–0), it was an enlightening experience to be in the dressing room for the pre-match team talk, at half time and at full time.

The U's followed up the 4–0 win over Bury Town with another victory on the road the following Saturday away at Bishop Stortford, 4–2. This was their final pre-season game. All in all, it hadn't been a bad pre-season; the players were beginning to gel and the new lads were fitting in. There had been a few frustrating knocks and injuries picked up, but there was a good atmosphere and buzz about the place. There was a quiet confidence that this would be a decent season – not a title-winning season, but a continued improvement on the tenth-placed finish of the 2009/10 season. And having seen a little bit of the team in action, and watching them in training, I shared that optimism.

The following Monday I was at the club again. First up was a meeting with Ian Darler and the police over the incident during the Leyton Orient game. This was simply a matter of going over what had occurred and reporting the various conversations that had taken place.

This particular morning had also been designated as the time to take the team photos and individual players' photos that would be used on the website and in programmes throughout the season. With the scholars also being required to be there for the CRC team photo, there was a lot of banter as the squads were suitably arranged. It was fascinating to watch to be honest – we needed photos with both the home and away kits, and of course not all the kit had arrived, so there were players hiding at the back wearing the wrong colour shorts and stress levels were rising. Watching how folk reacted was enlightening – some laughed it all off, some got wound up and others were totally oblivious to what was happening! But the end product was all very professional and you would never know the challenges taking the photos had brought.

This was again one of those times when I was hanging about with purpose – the 'ministry of presence' I referred to last month. I wasn't required to be there as I didn't have a particular role to fulfil, but I was there and was able to be seen to be present and to be around. Being visible is important in the role of chaplain. Very little of my time is actually spent talking to people about my faith and what I believe. However, the groundwork that is put in earning the right to be there, becoming an accepted face, and someone known to be part of the banter (as well as a target for it), means that when moments do come to talk about what I believe, it comes much more naturally as part of the conversation. I would love to have the opportunity to share my faith more, but in order to win the right to do that, being there to watch the team photos being taken and collecting the balls at training are essential first steps.

Following on from the photo shoot, the first team players trained. Well, when I say train, I was actually watching them take the Yo-Yo fitness test. This test requires the participants to run a given distance to a beep, turn and run back and then have a short recovery before repeating. It is continuous and the participants are not allowed to fall behind the beep otherwise they are out. The lads had taken this test at the start of pre-season and this was being repeated to see how their fitness levels had improved during the previous weeks of training.

Watching on, I was struck by how much the players encouraged each other. In the six seasons of being involved as chaplain, this was the most obvious I could remember it being, and it was apparent to me looking on that it started from the top. All of the management team were part of it, encouraging, being vocal and pushing the players to achieve. And the players that Martin had brought in were also playing a key role – they were a positive influence on the training ground. One might imagine that taking part in the Yo-Yo fitness test doesn't necessarily lend itself to lots of talking and encouragement, but as the players looked on and saw their team-mates starting to struggle, the encouragement came, and there was a pat on the back at the end too. And of course, it wouldn't have been right if there had been no banter and a few wisecracks!

But it struck me again how little in life we actually hear encouragement and a 'well done'. Even if it seems trivial and mundane, a thank you, a 'well done', a 'keep going', can make such a difference. This challenged me in my role as a leader in the Church, as a husband, a father and a friend. It is all too easy to be quick to criticise and pull people up when they get it wrong. For sure, we do need to deal with negative behaviour sometimes, but for this to occur in a healthy, positive environment can only help.

And interestingly enough, the Bible, particularly the New Testament, which is full of instructions on how to build a church community, is also full of expressions of togetherness such as 'one another' or 'let us'. It is sobering to remember that the Church is meant to be a place where people feel encouraged, supported, loved and accepted, where there is a genuine sense of community – and yet that often isn't people's experience of it. In my role, as I engage with people from wildly differing backgrounds, I hope that they experience from me something of what the Church should really be.

That evening we hosted a barbecue for the scholars at our home. This has become something that we have tried to do each year at least once, as it provides an opportunity for the lads to come and have something to eat and for me to get to know them outside of the footballing environment. Our own four lads, Kieran, Curtis, Jordan and Corban, soon get the scholars playing on the trampoline or the Wii.

The first years have left school at the end of June following their exams, and come the beginning of July they are living in digs and part of a professional football club, while many of their mates are still on holiday. College doesn't start until the beginning of September, so to be able to get out of the digs for an evening is for some a welcome relief. So we simply cook up some food, and let the lads chat, eat and relax. To be able to talk to the first years about where they have come from, their footballing background, what positions they play, and to find out a bit about their family, is all helpful in seeking to help them understand my role and the support I hope to be able to offer.

This season, with the large number of players that have come through the youth set-up within the first team squad, it was good to remember that only a few years ago, these lads were round our house for food – Josh Coulson, Robbie Willmott, Adam Marriott and Rory McAuley, for example, have all been part of these social times for the scholars, and as a result, my relationship with them is relaxed. They have never known there not to be a chaplain – it is an accepted part of their experience at Cambridge United.

So we will continue to seek these opportunities – maybe at Christmas we would have another social, depending on their training schedules. In the early years, we had also had a lunch for the first team squad – maybe it was time to put that on again.

One of the questions I get asked most pre-seasons by some of the lads is 'Did you have a good holiday?' Professional footballers, as I have already mentioned, get all of their holiday in one lump – usually a large part of May and most of June. For a lot of the other staff at the club, the close season is also a time for holidays, but for me with kids in school, I am still very much governed by school holidays. So it is that my main summer holiday usually coincides with the start of the football season, and this year was no different. The plan was for two weeks' off although we would only be away from Cambridge for the second week, so I would be able to be at the two home games in the first week of the season.

It is always a difficult one – technically, my role at the club is 'work' as the church I lead, Barnwell Baptist Church, are very good at releasing me to this work as chaplain, and they embrace it as part of my role at the church. So officially, when I am off work, I shouldn't be 'working' at the club. The reality for me is that I find my work as chaplain energising (most of the time!) and being a football fan anyway, it is something I enjoy. So my usual policy if we are around at home will be to attend the games but not be involved during the week while on holiday.

So for me, getting ready for a holiday was the focus of that week leading up to the start of the season, and that meant I needed to write four sets of programme notes because of timings and deadlines. This also included getting details together for the various charities we were working with as part of the Smile Scheme.

I was first contacted about programme notes a couple of years after I started. At that time I was asked if I would write an article for the Christmas and Easter programmes. The next season I did the same and the year after, I was asked to contribute more regularly. Not wanting to commit to something that I couldn't maintain or that wouldn't be received well, I agreed to write in about a third of the programmes and for the Christian festivals of Christmas and Easter. The following season I was asked to contribute to each programme, something I have been doing ever since, and this is something I enjoy and look forward to (most of the time!)

What do I write about? Well I try to respond to what is happening at the club, or to issues arising in the world of sport, entertainment or sometimes current affairs. Sometimes I will be more explicitly Christian and sometimes it is more of a moral challenge. In the four sets of notes that I wrote for the start of this season, for example, in two I didn't mention God at all, in the other two I was more open and direct in what I said.

For the Crawley game I wrote about the encouragement Mo Farah gave to his fellow Briton in the European Athletics championship, and the need in all of us to be encouraged and encourage one another. For Southport I wrote a piece about success and failure and how these can develop our characters. For the Eastbourne game I wrote about our community links as a club, and for Gateshead I wrote about how Christians are portrayed in the media, commenting on the series *Rev* and the portrayal of a Christian minister in the *EastEnders* storyline.

I am always on the lookout for quotes, anecdotes, stories or illustrations that I can use as the basis for my notes. When writing, I hope to make people think – whether it be about the need to encourage, or to say thank you as I did in one set of notes last season; or perhaps to think about their perception of the Church or Christianity. I have on a couple of occasions had people get in touch as a result of these notes – one particular fan wanted help in finding a local church to attend. I was able to help out, and still keep in contact with him, usually by text, email or phone as he's not based in Cambridge.

I am very privileged to have this opportunity and, as with other aspects of my role, I don't wish to abuse it. However, I do wish to be true to who I am and unashamed of what I believe. I hoped as the season went by to make the most of these opportunities.

The league fixture schedule is so arranged that by the end of September a quarter of the season has been played. The reason for this is that once the various cup competitions start games need to be rearranged due to replays, for example. It also recognises that during most winters there will be games postponed due to the weather often leading to frosty or waterlogged pitches. As it turned out, a considerable number of games in the 2010/11 season were postponed due to the cold weather and snow we had.

Even allowing for this, there are usually a couple of teams in the league that still end up with a fixture backlog and a fairly heavy run-in at the end of the season, which can prove significant in terms of deciding who finishes where. For example, a part-time team having to play on a Saturday, Tuesday, Thursday, and then another Saturday for a couple of weeks can have a big effect, not only on their own finishing league position, but also on that of teams that play them during this spell.

So the fixtures come thick and fast in the early weeks of the season. For the 2010/11 season the club had played six games by the end of August, three home and three away, with a midweek game as well as the Saturday fixture each week.

For a player, it does mean that if you are out for a couple of weeks you can potentially miss four games, whereas in the mid-season with just Saturday fixtures you'll maybe only miss a couple. This becomes all the more important when you have a small squad of players to work with. Recovery time between games is short and fitness levels need to be up so that you can hit the ground running from the first game of the season – this is why pre-season is such a significant time.

Pre-season was now over and the real business began with the first game of the season – an away fixture with Wrexham. I mentioned earlier that I like to get to some away games during the course of the season. These tend to be the evening games, as I work on Sundays and this means I can have the occasional Saturday with the family. However, if I can, I'll be tuned in to Johno and Lino (Mark Johnson and Steve Line) on BBC Radio Cambridgeshire with their live commentary and witty analysis.

It was a disappointing start to the season for the U's: a 1–0 defeat. The team played well and deserved to get something out of the game by all accounts, Dean Saunders, the Wrexham manager conceding that towards the end of the game, Wrexham were hanging on. Dave Partridge, who started at centre back, was knocked out at the end of the first half and replaced at half-time – he subsequently missed a number of games because of their frequency during the month.

Although United came away with no points from their trip to North Wales, there was still a sense of optimism at the ground for the first home game of the season, a tasty little encounter with big-spending Crawley Town, with a management duo of Steve Evans and assistant Paul Raynor (who used to play at United) – two of the more lively characters you'll see pitchside in the Blue Square Bet Premier Division!

But what does a match day look like for me? I usually try to get to the ground an hour and a half before kick-off, a little less for an evening match. I have a routine that I follow – first of all I check in to the club offices to collect my match-day pass, programme and any notes. I also check in with the club secretary to see if there is anything I need to be aware of. From there I usually head to the dressing room to shake the players' hands and wish them well before they go out for warm-up, and this will also take in the management team, physio, kit man and club doctor. My next stop is with the stadium manager, where I pick up the microphone and check if there is anything they need or want to let me know about. Occasionally, there will be something happening on the pitch at half-time, for example, a penalty shoot-out or presentation, and I need to check that Ian and the stewards are aware of this.

From there I will head up to speak to the other tannoy announcer who sits at the back of the main stand, operates the music and gives out safety announcements, birthdays, scorers and so on. I check which announcements he has and which I have to make sure we know what we're doing. From there I visit the media area to say a quick hello to the radio commentators, and then go to the hospitality area to see if there is anything I need to be aware of from their end. I will also introduce myself to the match-day mascot if there is one.

Between twenty-five and twenty minutes before kick-off I will give everyone a welcome to the game, encourage them to get their programmes and make any other announcements, for example, giving information about the Smile Scheme charity of the day. Once the teams leave after their warm-up, about 15 minutes before kick-off, I will repeat the welcome and notices and then read out the names of the players from the team sheet I have been given. I will then make my way to the tunnel where I wait for the teams to assemble and then welcome the teams to the pitch. They then gather at the halfway line for the Respect handshake. The Football Association's RESPECT campaign has seen the handshake, which has been seen at international games and Champions' League fixtures for many years, filter down to the grassroots. It is now a feature of matches in the non-league set-up; both teams line up on either side of the officials, and pass in single file shaking hands with everyone.

I run through the teams again before leaving the pitch. From there, I usually go to the dressing room – the substitutes are usually still there, having just finished their warm-up and left the pitch as the two teams walk out. There they will get their kit – shin pads, shirt, jackets in winter and some water, before they head to the dugout. And sometimes the injured players and others not involved haven't made their way to the stand either.

I have no designated seat, so I am free to move about and will do so depending on what is happening, who is around, if there are people I want to catch up with. It does give me some flexibility.

Despite all the optimism, the game against Crawley didn't start well, the U's finding themselves 2–0 down after 10 minutes. However, they showed great discipline and determination, eventually coming back to 2–2 by half-time. With no score in the second half, the spoils were shared.

One of the features of life in the Conference, and particularly at a club like United with its recent history, is that so many players have passed through the changing rooms in recent seasons. There are a number of factors causing the high turnover of players in Conference level football. The first is that players from league clubs – either youth team players just breaking through, or more established players who are sitting on the bench or recovering from injury – drop down to the Conference to get games under their belt. These may be short-term loans, sometimes for a month at a time. Some of the more experienced players who are moving towards the end of their careers are more interested in trying to find a football club that is closer to home rather than playing at the highest level they possibly can – it does have financial implications, but for many of these players their values have changed a little and time with family has become more important.

Another factor is that some players at Conference level are working up from part-time non-league teams. They then get spotted and offered a contract at a professional non-league team. Some of these players then go on again to play in the Football League, but more often than not these players peak at this level.

And the other major factor at Conference level are the financial constraints on many clubs which prohibit the offering of long-term contracts, and so players do tend to move round a little bit more. It has been the norm for example at United to have contracts that are no longer than a year, or perhaps two years at most.

At United, our situation is a little different to many of the clubs at this level. When I was first appointed as chaplain back in 2005, the club, coming out of administration, had four players on contract and this was only weeks before the season started. So quite a number of players came through in those early days on trial, and in that first season the club had about 45 different players who played in the first team. This pattern continued the next season and then began to stabilise. The other contributing factor at United has been the change of managers, with each manager having a slightly different style and looking for a slightly different profile of player.

So each managerial change has seen a few leave and a few come in. Often those arriving at the club initially do so on loan – some players stay and others leave.

So it's very rare for a team to arrive at United without an ex-United player among their ranks, and there will often be an opportunity for me to shake their hand and offer a quick 'Hello, how's it going?' With Crawley there were three players – Jai Reason, Liam Enver-Marum and Scott Neilson – who had previously worn the amber and black. Jai had been released at the end of the previous season, and Scott had been on loan from Bradford City for the last few games of the previous season as well. However, I didn't get the chance to speak to them that evening.

Next up after Crawley, the following Saturday, was another home game against newly promoted Southport. This was one of those frustrating afternoons when they came and played with ten men behind the ball and sat and defended doggedly. I have lost count of the number of games in recent seasons where the opposition have adopted that strategy. We just could not break them down, leaving the fans with a disappointing 0–0 draw at full time.

Reflecting on the two games I had seen so far, the players hadn't played badly at all, but the final pass wasn't quite going to feet, or the final ball was a little over-hit or the player had mistimed their run. It was often just fine margins, and bearing in mind that a number of new players had been brought together it was to be expected. Even though pre-season had been good, there was still work to do, but time would see things slotting into place and as the players got more used to each other, I hoped the results will come.

Although I was officially 'on holiday', I took a phone call from one of the players who rang me to talk about something that was happening at home. During the whole conversation he was concerned about who I might tell and asked me to promise not to pass this on. This is critical for the chaplain – I should be somebody that players, management, staff and supporters can talk to confidentially, without that conversation being reported to anyone, unless necessary. As I am not part of the management team, an employee of the club, nor a director, my role is independent from them, and occasionally someone will speak to me about something that is going on in their lives – something that they don't want others to know about. Of course, wisdom (and the law!) does dictate that at times, the information shared does need to be reported on, but in those situations it should be done preferably with the person's knowledge.

And while the chaplain is independent, they are at the same time also dependent on the relationships they share with managers, players and others to add value to the work of the club. My experiences have been varied – the four managers I have experienced have all been welcoming – although the last two managers Gary Brabin and Martin Ling have been more open to my presence in the dressing room, for example.

To me, being in that place of trust is a particular privilege and honour – I do not take lightly the fact that occasionally people will open up to me about all manner of things. At the same time, it can be a challenge. There have been times over the past five seasons where I have had fans, directors, management and staff all talk to me about the same issue, but I am not at liberty to pass on information I have got from other conversations! I simply have to listen and then encourage them to either talk to someone else, or accept that they may not have the whole story.

In the course of my work and ministry at the club, there are times when I become party to confidential information, but I need to recognise that my role requires of me that I am impartial and accessible to all. However, I know that for some this makes things difficult – some chaplains have found themselves in very difficult situations in other contexts. I can remember one occasion where a staff member asked me to be their witness in a meeting they had with the club over a matter, and I decided to decline as I felt it would be very difficult for me to be on one side of the table or the other. My support needed to be available for both parties. Other chaplains I know would take a different line and a different approach, but at that time and in that context, this was the decision I reached and I still think it was the right one.

I was able to follow up the phone conversation I'd had with the player when I got back from the holiday and was really pleased that the matter was resolved.

Next up was an away fixture with Tamworth – being on holiday, I couldn't get to hear it on the radio, and had to make do with buying the paper the next morning. A point away from home wasn't a bad result, although the report indicated that we were in control until a lapse of concentration in the last ten minutes gifted them the equaliser.

The following weekend was the August Bank Holiday weekend, with a disappointing performance leading to a 1–0 defeat at Mansfield on the Saturday, followed up by a much more convincing 2–0 first win of the season against Eastbourne at home on Bank Holiday Monday. With the former U's captain, Danny Brown, in the Eastbourne line-up, it was a good win. It was also good to catch up with him afterwards and ask after his family.

So the month ended with the first win of the new campaign and statistics of: played 6, won 1, drawn 3, lost 2, We finished in 17th place in the table – not a great start perhaps, but certainly the potential was there for the team to push on. Some of Martin Ling's acquisitions were looking very useful and there was no doubt that we would see much more of them in the coming weeks.

Off the pitch, the Smile Scheme had had a positive start, with just over £900 raised over the three league games and last pre-season game against Leyton Orient. In September, with the schools back, and my more regular working schedule kicking in, the year would get properly under way.

August Results

Sat 14	Blue Square Bet Premier	**Wrexham 1 United 0**
Tues 17	Blue Square Bet Premier	**United 2 Crawley Town 2** *Russell, Saah*
Sat 21	Blue Square Bet Premier	**United 0 Southport 0**
Tues 24	Blue Square Bet Premier	**Tamworth 1 United 1** *Wright*
Sat 28	Blue Square Bet Premier	**Mansfield Town 1 United 0**
Mon 30	Blue Square Bet Premier	**United 2 Eastbourne Borough 0** *Coulson, Jennings*

September 2010

The month began with our home game against Gateshead. Unfortunately, missing from the line-up was one of Martin Ling's summer signings, Adam Miller, who was suffering from an injured ankle following a full-blooded tackle with former U's captain Danny Brown in the Eastbourne game. That would be Adam's last contribution on the field in his first season for the club – a huge disappointment for all involved, as the team was just beginning to look settled.

Another of the new boys, Daryl Clare, had an 18th-minute penalty saved against the club he had ended the previous season playing for. However, the U's took the lead just nine minutes later, and went on to record a 5–0 victory. It was a good performance all round and pleasing for all concerned that things seemed to be gelling.

In football, there are some games where things just seem to work; everything you do comes off, and when those games coincide with the fact that the opposite is true for the opposition, that is when you get big scores. It was a bit like the 6–0 win for Ipswich against Manchester United back in the eighties or the 9–0 the other way a few seasons back. This was one of those games – the chances we had we took. It did bring confidence, but equally it was important not to get carried away and think that we would be trouncing teams every week. As had already been proved in the first few games of the season, and also in previous seasons, the Blue Square Bet Conference Premier is a hard league to get out of and there are very few, if any, weak teams.

Now that the school holidays were finished, my weekly schedule began to fall into place, and that involved me attending the training ground on Monday mornings. This would become my regular time to meet up with the players and management. So, it was off to

Pembroke College sports ground, only to discover that the first team had the day off! After seven games in three weeks, and with no midweek game, the schedules had altered.

As I am not part of the management team, I don't always get to hear when things have changed, and to be fair, I'm not on the top of the list of people to phone when the schedules change and nor should I be! This is something I've learned to live with – in previous seasons, when the first team had a different training facility each day, there were a handful of occasions when I would spend all morning driving round the various grounds they used and not find them! There has been more than one occasion when my morning set aside to watch the players train has ended with frustration. Fortunately, with the new arrangement to use Clare College's training ground, and the combination of the first team and scholars sharing the facilities, the chances were there wouldn't be many occasions when I would be greeted by an empty field.

The morning wasn't wasted though, as after a quick car journey to Clare College sports ground, I discovered that the scholars were training and it meant I was able to watch them and catch up with Jez George and Nolan Keeley. After watching the lads train, I stayed on as they had their lunch to have a cup of coffee and to be around. Again, it was one of those times where I might get a ten-second conversation with one of the lads about their weekend, or about Saturday's game – very short and sweet, but nonetheless essential as part of building friendship and trust with them. The scholars have always been taught by Jez to show respect and they will all come and shake my hand.

The following Saturday saw the U's lose 2–0 away to Luton. This was disappointing but not altogether unexpected as Luton were one of the fancied teams for promotion in the 2010/11 season. One of the negatives from that game was an injury picked up by another of Martin's summer signings, Conal Platt, which would rule him out for a few weeks. That meant that three of Martin's summer signings had now been injured – how frustrating for him that the players he had brought in to strengthen and build the squad were those ending up on the physio's couch! But that is the reality of the game of football. You can pay silly money for a top professional only for them to pick up a serious injury in their first game for the club, ending their career. It is a risk that is taken when the money is paid out. Unfortunately, you can't wrap them in cotton wool!

On the next Monday I headed back to Clare College – Martin Ling was not there as he wasn't well, so John Schofield was taking the training. Conal was still resting and would be at home for the first few days while the injury settled before coming in to see Greg and have it assessed before starting treatment and rehab. Daryl Clare was also still working with Greg to get himself fit.

Over the time I have been chaplain, some of the best relation-ships I have shared with players have been those born out of spending time with them while they are sidelined, receiving treat-ment and following surgery. Perhaps they themselves are a little more relaxed, a little less focused on playing; perhaps they feel a little more vulnerable and that causes them to open up a bit. So looking out for the players who are sidelined, keeping in touch via text messages and sitting with them in the stand during matches, are all ways of supporting them.

There is nothing more encouraging than someone taking a genu-ine interest in you. I'm sure many of us can relate to the experience of talking with someone who is either distracted by someone or something else and is not paying attention, or looks for every opportunity to turn the conversation back round to them. Those are the kind of conversations that you walk away from wondering why you bother! I'm sure we can all think of people that are like that – always want to talk about themselves, or always seemingly uninter-ested – but I guess we also need to ask ourselves whether we can be like that at times too.

The Bible is full of really helpful advice. It is sad that it receives so much bad and negative press – if only people would pick it up and take a look, they would find loads of really down-to-earth, practical advice to help us in our lives and in our relationships. To give an example, Philippians 2:3–4 says: 'In humility value others above yourselves, not looking to your own interests but each of you to the interests of the others.' If only people lived like that, wouldn't our society, our world, our communities and families be a much nicer place to be? And yet, we also know that at our core, we can be quite selfish and self-centred – looking after number one. The Bible isn't simply made up of a list of rules and regulations, it provides a template for life, and as a Christian, it is my desire that I may increasingly be more like Jesus and live my life more by his standards.

And that includes the way I am with people. The more I understand about someone, the more I know about their family situation, their career, their life, the more I am able to empathise with them, to help and support them and to be the best friend I can to them. So times like the one I shared with Daryl that day are precious as they help me gather information that I store away to help in building a relationship. I genuinely seek to take an interest in the people I meet, to take the time to listen to them and to log away relevant and important information. There is nothing more annoying than trying to have a conversation with someone who only wants to talk about themselves, and I don't ever want to be that person!

For me, it is important that my life is consistent, that the way I conduct myself is not simply about a professional code of conduct, but it is a way of life based on the Bible that I seek to follow and be obedient to – whether that be at church, at the club or at home. Do I do that all the time? Not at all! In fact, I get it wrong more often than I get it right. But, with God's help, I seek to become more like him each day.

Interestingly, at the training ground that morning I also got the opportunity for a longer conversation with Jez George that wasn't driven by football results or performances, training schedules and the like. In Jez's situation, he finds himself juggling many responsibilities as manager of the youth team and director of football. It is a challenging and, at times, difficult role with the scholars because he is their manager and he wants to improve their footballing ability and career potential. But above everything else, although Jez is focused on developing footballing talent, he is most concerned at developing young men. So in many ways, he finds himself almost acting as a parent for them, helping them talk through their problems, watching over them in their digs, making sure things are done well and properly and trying at arm's length to keep their domestic arrangements ticking over.

He does all this while trying to raise funds, because the club gets no financial support from the footballing authorities for its youth development work as Cambridge United is not a league club. This is a cause Jez has been championing with Premier League and Football Association officials for the past few years, raising the matter with the national press and on Sky Sports News and programmes like Soccer AM. He has also sought to get some of the top professionals to lend their support – ex-Cambridge United player Dave Kitson, for example, has been very supportive of the cause. There are signs that light is beginning to appear at the end of the tunnel, but how quickly any financial benefit, if any at all, will be realised is yet to be known.

After training, I hung around over a cup of coffee as the players got changed and had their lunch. Once Jez and Nolan have got the lads off the training pitch, they focus on their development off the field – any discipline issues, anyone not pulling their weight in the digs, anyone not bringing their kit with them, finding out who is cooking lunch and making drinks and so on. The time I get to spend sat around drinking a coffee and being part of the banter and experience is all part of making myself available and accessible.

Later that week, I was at the club for a meeting with Martin Jordan to review how the Smile Scheme had been going and to look at requests that had been received and how we could respond to them – some of these requests had been submitted by fans, and some had been received through the office. The take-up had been very positive, and by the end of the meeting, the season was pretty well covered with a mix of local and national charities, one-off collections and links with national initiatives. We also had a conversation with the commercial manager, Claudine Bone, and club secretary, Lisa Baldwin, asking them if we could have the charity of the day listed on the official team sheets, and if the charity collectors could have access to the hospitality area.

The charity collections were being run as part of the work of the newly formed Cambridge United Youth and Community Trust. This was a new development, and linked in with the work Jez was doing with the scholars, and the work that cascaded down from that, although in reality the club also benefited, as the scholars themselves are the end product of a lot of work with a lot of young people across a wide area. The establishing of the Trust has been a massive step forward in tying together the work being done by the youth development team in coaching youngsters from seven and eight through to the scholars at 16–18 with the work done in schools – teaching, lunchtime and after schools clubs. There is also a lot of other work that the club is developing as part of its work in the community.

The appointment of Nigel Ashman to develop this work was a step forward, and a step into the unknown. Funding for youth development is uncertain and has to be raised, as has been mentioned already, but community work presents a much more attractive option for sponsorship, and the charity collections and donations demonstrated tangible evidence that the Trust was giving to the local community. As the season progressed, and my community involvement also moved forward, I expected I would be linking up more with Nigel.

The U's next game was away to Kidderminster – a trip I had also made back in March with the team. The lads' returned with a point following a 0–0 draw. While a little disappointing, it was largely accepted as a fair result as neither team really created the chances. From United's point of view, having got to the end of August with a team that was beginning to look settled and the new players beginning to gel, suddenly Martin was facing selection changes for most games and a constant juggling act in deciding the best positions for each player and how to move them around in order to get the best out of them individually and collectively.

As chaplain, one of the privileges I have from time to time is to be invited to speak about what I do to different groups. A number of these opportunities crop up through the course of a season and in the past have led me to speak at luncheon clubs, men's breakfasts, supper evenings, and a Rotary group. On this occasion, I was invited to speak to the King's School assembly. The King's School is one of the top independent schools in the country and is situated in the shadow of Ely Cathedral, which is where the assembly itself takes place. The assembly comprises a procession in, a short five to ten minute talk, a prayer, a hymn led by the choir and a procession out.

It was an honour to be able to share briefly about what I do and why I do it. As I've mentioned already, the very nature of the work I do and the ministry I am involved in means that very often my contact time is minimal and so I seek to make the most of every opportunity.

So in approaching this assembly I wanted to include something that would be of interest to the students – inviting a football club chaplain to speak, they will naturally want to hear some anecdotal material about the role; but at the same time I wanted to challenge them about their perception of the Church and ultimately God – how does belief in God align with a passion for football? I also believe strongly that the Bible can really change lives – often the problem is it isn't explained properly or is presented in a drab and boring way. So I always try to introduce some part of the Bible when I'm speaking. These opportunities are not simply about entertainment, although I hope that people find an element of that, but to leave people with something to think about as well.

If you knew that you only had five minutes left before you drew your final breath, what would be the words you would want to speak in those five minutes? You would want to say words that counted and that meant something. It may sound morbid but that is how I try to view life – to make the most of every moment, to make the most of every opportunity – that is primarily why I accepted the invitation to write this book. To use the well rehearsed words spoken by Robin Williams in the film *Dead Poets Society*: 'Carpe diem. Seize the day, boys. Make your lives extraordinary.'

In my life and work, this means recognising that every day, in fact every breath I take, is a gift from God, and I therefore choose to live my life in a way that I hope honours him. For me, seizing the day is trying to show and tell people about God, although I know I am guilty of too much 'showing' and not enough 'telling'. The assembly was encouraging and a pleasure to be able to share in. I trust that God will take the words spoken and remind the students of those words as the days, months and years roll on.

As I have described the way my role has evolved, it is apparent that I am seen to be a good link with other opportunities for the club to connect with the local community. One of the ways this has happened in the last couple of years is through linking in with a partnership called Cambridgeshire Celebrates Age (CCA) which exists to promote well-being among the older generation. It does this through promoting activities, creating working partnerships, providing information, and trying to challenge misconceptions of older people in society. This partnership produces a programme of events for the month of October, to coincide with the International Day of Older People on 1 October.

I got involved initially through my links with the local churches as many of them have active groups for this age group, but weren't being represented in this partnership. But while there, and wearing my Cambridge United chaplain's hat, I was able to create a link between the two, which has seen the club have a Seniors Day for the past two seasons (those over 65 can get in at a much reduced rate) and also host the CCA programme press launch.

It has become increasingly obvious to me over the past few seasons that to get the attention of the press, you do need to be a little creative, and the local press do like Cambridge United. So for the past two years, holding the press launch at the club has helped CCA to get some decent coverage in the local press, which it was unable to do before.

Following the assembly in Ely, it was back to the club to play host to the 2010 press launch, to welcome the various dignitaries that were present (following this visit by the Mayor, she was invited back as guest of honour to a future home game) and seeking to build on the club's relationships with the various agencies represented at the press launch.

The U's played host to Kettering next, United looking for their first win in three games and trying to extend their winning home run, which they managed with a 3–0 win. After the game, I had the opportunity to speak to the Kettering assistant manager Tommy Jaszczun, another who used to play for the U's, and to catch up on how he and his family were doing.

Later that week, I hosted a meeting at the church at which we had members of the Cambridge Fans United (CFU) committee and Ariadne Henry who works for Cambridge City Council as their Equalities Development Project Worker. She in turn brought with her the Chief Officer of the Cambridge Ethnic Community Forum, Eddie Stadnik.

Further to the conversation I had with the Chairman of CFU in the summer, one of the initiatives I had suggested that made sense for CFU to embrace was the link with the Black and Minority Ethnic groups in Cambridge. By and large, our fan base is of White British ethnicity and doesn't therefore tend to reach into what is a significant group within Cambridge. I had met Ariadne on a number of occasions and we had often spoken about working to link Cambridge United with these groups and the best way forward to do that.

The club had participated in the 'Kick It Out' campaigns in previous years, but had not been so good at following through with the initiative in making links locally. The 'Let's Kick Racism out of Football' campaign was started in 1993 and has been running ever since. In 1997 'Kick It Out' was established and in 2001, the first 'Kick It Out' week of action took place. Each year since, this national campaign encourages football clubs to participate, now under the banner 'One Game, One Community', and has grown beyond simply tackling the issue of racism to cover all areas of prejudice and discrimination – race, religion, age, gender, disability and sexual orientation. (For more information go to the 'Kick It Out' website – www.kickitout.org.)

So this meeting, while having a specific game in mind to raise the profile of the campaign and to hand out flyers and stickers, was more about opening up lines of communication to enable the club to be more active within the community of Cambridge. It proved to be a profitable time and the 'Kick It Out' game was fixed for October and other matters like involving the press were highlighted to be addressed. Nick Parker, one of the CFU committee members, took responsibility for pulling it all together and making it happen. The next challenge will be for the club to work on achieving the Equality Standard, and it may be that this is an area that I offer to help the club develop.

We also hosted a coffee morning at our church as part of the World's Biggest Coffee Morning fundraising campaign run by Macmillan Cancer Support. In recent years we have managed to tie this event in with the players' training schedule so that they are able to join us for a cup of tea or coffee and a piece of cake before heading off to the training ground. This enables us to raise the profile of the event, to welcome more locals along and to raise more money – all of which is great news!

We have also had with us for the last two years children from Fen Ditton Community Primary School, where I serve as a governor. The children come along and entertain us with songs and poems. It was great this year to see a number of the players interacting with the children, encouraging them, joining in and being part of the event for what it was, rather than simply because they'd been told to come along. In fact, three of the lads who had arrived late for training that morning were 'gently encouraged' to join the school children in singing Paul Simon's 'Call me Al', which was a great buzz for the children and added to the atmosphere of the morning. They were then joined by Danny Naisbitt as they sang 'La Bamba'.

This event, while being great fun, is a good way to raise funds and engage with the community, and also gives an opportunity for the players to see the church where I am minister and to meet other members of the church.

The day after the coffee morning, the U's were again in action at home, playing host to newly promoted Newport County. Their manager, Dean Holdsworth, had had a month on loan playing at United a couple of seasons earlier, so it was good to make contact with him, along with another ex-United lad, Daryl Knights. Daryl had been on loan with the U's from Yeovil to be near to his family because of a family situation that had arisen – his family were from Ipswich, and so it was good to see him again and find out how things were there.

Unfortunately matters on the pitch weren't so great on that afternoon as we lost 1–0. Newport scored in the second minute and then sat back and defended, as many teams have at the Abbey. We were simply unable to break them down.

Later that afternoon, I bumped into Dave Coulson, the father of one of the players, Josh, who I have got to know through the work at the club. Dave told me that only that morning, Josh's gran had been found dead at home. This was only months after his granddad had died under very similar circumstances. They had not told Josh the news – they were waiting to break it to him after the game. The family are close and losing his granddad had hit Josh hard. It was a privilege to be there at that moment and to offer some support to the family. I was able to keep in touch with Josh over the next couple of days by text.

Text messaging has been a real blessing for me in keeping in touch with players, both those currently at the club and those who have moved on. I find it helpful because it isn't as intrusive as a phone call, and it leaves the player in a position where they can respond if they wish and not if they don't. The downside is that if they don't respond, you don't know if their number has changed or not! Often when players are injured I'll drop them a text if they have an operation coming up or afterwards, just to let them know I'm thinking of them and praying for them.

The following week I had a meeting at the Cambridge United Learning Centre. This had been established a few years before as a place for school students to attend if they needed a little extra tuition and perhaps would find the football club a good place to go for some extra input. Football, along with IT, is particularly used to give extra input for literacy and numeracy, but it's also an environment where the children can gain extra confidence.

Unfortunately, the funding looked set to be cut, and so I met with Helen Dyson, the new centre manager, to talk about what she has planned and how we could link in together. I had worked closely with her predecessor Jez Daniels, but had not had the opportunity until that time to meet up with Helen. There were lots of creative ideas, but in reality it was difficult to know how best to develop these when the future was uncertain and funding was likely to be cut at the end of the financial year in March 2011.

The month ended with an away trip to AFC Wimbledon and a 3–0 defeat. United finished the month with a record of: played 12, won 3, drawn 4, lost 5, and sat in 16th place in the table. It hadn't been great, but on the playing side the management and players were not too despondent as they believed in what they were doing and the resources available. The fans, however, were not feeling quite so positive and there were the beginnings of some rumblings of discontent.

I felt for Martin – his attempt to bring in players to add to what he already had in place hadn't worked out because of injuries. I was hoping and praying that things would get better!

September Results

Sat 4	Blue Square Bet Premier	**United 5 Gateshead 0**
		Wright, Clare, Russell, Saah, Gray
Sat 11	Blue Square Bet Premier	**Luton Town 2 United 0**
Sat 18	Blue Square Bet Premier	**Kidderminster Harriers 0 United 0**
Tues 21	Blue Bet Square Premier	**United 3 Kettering Town 0**
		Gray, Willmott, Wright
Sat 25	Blue Square Bet Premier	**United 0 Newport County 1**
Wed 29	Blue Bet Square Premier	**AFC Wimbledon 3 United 0**

October 2010

The footballing world is a very strange world and footballers are a strange breed! There is a lot of banter, bravado and testosterone – the changing room is certainly not a place for the faint-hearted. And yet there are times when all of that is taken away and you find that players are just as vulnerable as anyone else; they are equally prone to fear, worry and anxiety.

I have alluded to the moments after a player is injured and the vulnerability that they experience at that time. Like all of us, they may also face the loss of a loved one, concern for family and friends and anxiety about their career; in so many areas football players are vulnerable. The problem comes in how to deal with that – after all, you don't want to lose face or look weak in front of the rest of your team-mates. And if you talk to your manager, will he drop you – or worse, put you on the transfer list?

As a chaplain, these are the moments when being available matters – players know that they can get in touch and unload their worries, anxieties and fears without it going back to the changing room. With long-term injuries there can be anxieties about the future – will I ever play again? And if I do, will I have lost my touch, ability and speed? These questions can dominate a player's mind in the weeks after an injury occurs.

But there is also another, perhaps more subtle, difficulty that arises for those with long-term injuries – they are often out of the team environment for months. They miss out on the banter and the rapport. They still belong, but then again they don't, and they can become isolated, particularly if they are the only one in the treatment room. And these times present to the chaplain a good opportunity to become a friend, someone who will ring and text to see how they are doing while they are sitting at home for weeks on end.

Adam Miller, who suffered a nasty ankle injury in the game against Eastbourne, had spent September working on his rehab – would the ankle repair itself, or would it require surgery? By the end of the month it was apparent that it would be the latter and so on

1 October, 'Millsy' had his operation. On the Saturday morning, I popped in to see him. He was still snoring his head off, but later woke up and we spent a good bit of time chatting about his career, his family and his views on Christianity and the Church. The surgery was pretty extensive and would mean he would be in a cast and then a boot for a good 10–12 weeks.

Being a more senior player, he was perhaps more philosophical about his situation than others may have been. The other thing he had to his advantage was that he was on a three year contract and so although he would be missing the rest of the season, he still had a contract to come back to.

However, other players are not so lucky, and an injury as you come towards the end of your contract can render you unemployed and unemployable. These are the times when having a friend that isn't required to balance the books or produce performances and results on the pitch is so helpful, and all those times of sitting around with a coffee, watching the training session in the rain and collecting the balls from the hedges and ditches pays off.

That afternoon, back at the Abbey, there was another home game, this time against another newly promoted side, Bath City. They also boasted three ex-United players, although only one from my time at the club – Lee Phillips, who had been released at the end of the previous season. While it was good to catch up with him and hear how he was doing, the result wasn't so great, with Bath scoring a late winner to claim a 2–1 away win and condemn the U's to their second successive home defeat, by a newly promoted side we were expected to beat, comfortably in some people's eyes.

So it was that the players and management headed off down the tunnel to the dressing room to the sound of boos and chants of 'Ling out'. Football is a funny old game, as one Jimmy Greaves used to say. It is also very fickle – you can go from hero to zero in a week and vice versa. There are very few managers who have brought instant success to a club, and even fewer who have managed to sustain it.

By my sixth season as chaplain, I had seen some strange comings and goings at the club, and I had got to know players, staff, directors, fans and managers over that time. It can be a painful place to be, stuck in the middle, and at times that is how it feels. That afternoon, sitting in the stand watching the players and management leave the pitch and listening to the fans was hard. Having access to the players and management, I understood what they were trying to do and how they were struggling with issues beyond their control. Yet the reality was that the performances to this point hadn't been good enough – the team were not playing to their potential and the fans who had paid their hard-earned money to watch the football had a point.

Things only got worse that week, with a Tuesday night trip to Hayes & Yeading and another dismal display, the hosts winning 2–0. The only upside was that it was away from home, so there were fewer U's fans there to see it and react!

I happened to be away that week. I have already mentioned that as part of my chaplaincy work I had linked up with SCORE, the national Sports chaplains' network. Twice a year SCORE chaplains meet in regional groupings and in October they have a 48-hour conference, spread over three days. This is where I was, sharing some time with other football chaplains, from premiership clubs right down through to the non-league pyramid, and with chaplains from county cricket, Rugby Union and League, athletics and horse racing.

I have always enjoyed these conferences as they are a time to network with others doing the same work, to learn from them and their experiences and opportunities, to ask after players that have moved between clubs and to receive some professional input into areas that it isn't easy to have addressed at local level. For example, Martyn Heather from the Premier League helped us think through some of the ethical issues facing football, and sport in general, and Christine Yorath, wife of Terry and mum to Gabby Logan, and Val Lumsden, wife of Jimmy, shared about the impact of their husbands' careers – both as players and then as part of the management at club and country level – on home life. This was very helpful and inspirational, and challenged us on how we could better support families. My experience at Cambridge United has been that players' wives and girlfriends do not attend that often, and many not at all. There are very few that actually live close to Cambridge and so our contact with them is minimal. And yet as Christine and Val were speaking the realisation dawned on me again that not only does their home situation have a big impact on the players and therefore the club, but what happens at the club has the potential to have a massive impact on things at home! And if that is the case, what implications does that have for me and my role?

Sheila Medici, who works with the Premier League as a Safeguarding consultant, led us through a very helpful session on safeguarding practices recommended by the Football Association. 'Safeguarding' is the term used to cover issues not just to do with protecting children (by definition under-18s) from potential abuse, but also with preventing such abuse. It also protects coaches and adults from the possibility of false accusations by agreeing and initiating good practice. This was particularly helpful when we began to look at particular scenarios and how we would respond in each one. For example, if a child (this would include one of the scholars under 18, who are still legally children) asks to be your friend on Facebook, should you accept or not? While not being a specific issue for me, as I don't have a Facebook account (my wife Hayley does and keeps me posted), it did raise some interesting discussion about appropriate boundaries for chaplains.

The final session was with Tony Spreadbury who spoke humorously about some of his experiences as a Rugby Union referee at the top of his sport, and offered some thoughts as to how chaplains could support referees, and other potential links between the two.

Alongside all of this, there was plenty of time to chat and to swap stories. And of course, there was the now infamous North v South football match. This year it was a 5-a-side match, which, sadly, the North won fairly convincingly.

I have developed some good contacts with some of the chaplains at other clubs, particularly at the level at which United are playing, and from time to time will get in touch to see if they are heading in our direction. If I am travelling with the team, I try to find out if they are going to be around to meet up.

I always come away from the conference with plenty to think about and reflect on, as I'm constantly seeking to improve the service I give as chaplain. But I'm also replaying some of the conversations and thinking about some of the clubs where chaplaincy isn't taking place.

Football is indeed a funny old game, and it is also a very small world. A week is a long time in football and a lot can change. The manager at your club one day is suddenly the manager at a different club the next – if his experience of chaplaincy has been good and there have been some good practices developed, this can pave the way for a chaplain at a club without one. Sadly the opposite is also true – if a good manager with a healthy relationship with the chaplain leaves, the door can be closed overnight to chaplaincy.

One of the clubs in the Conference Premier that do have a chaplain is Altrincham, and I get on really well with their chaplain, Andy. Although Andy wasn't able to be at the conference, we keep in regular email contact through the season, and the chaplains' conference and the regional meetings are always encouraging.

United's next game was another away game, this time against Fleetwood Town, another of the new teams in the league. They had come up as league winners from the Blue Square Bet Conference North the previous season and were rumoured to be 'flashing the cash' a little in an attempt to gain immediate promotion into the League. Fleetwood was a good four-hour journey up north, and in those situations the players usually travel up the day before and stay overnight – this would be the second time they had done this in the season, the first having been the opening day fixture away at Wrexham.

The game had been moved to the Sunday as it was being televised live, and was kicking off at the unhelpful time of 4.00 p.m. I say unhelpful, because for the travelling United contingent it would mean getting home an hour later on a Sunday evening – the original scheduled time of Saturday afternoon meant they would have had the Sunday to recover before heading back to work or school. For some, their planned weekend taking in a Saturday afternoon game, now had to change with the game being played 24 hours later – there were a number of unhappy fans at United as a result of that.

Under the eye of the TV cameras the U's put in a sterling performance to come away with a 2–2 draw. Loan player Alex Stavrinou, in from Charlton for a few weeks, scored the opening U's goal on his debut, seemingly immediately justifying Martin Ling's decision. The point was secured with a Robbie Willmott penalty after substitute Jordan Patrick had teased the Fleetwood defence into bringing him down – credit again to Martin Ling for introducing JP. This game would prove to be a significant one for the team in the coming weeks.

On the Tuesday after the game I attended the funeral of Josh's gran, just as I had his granddad's. While receiving a card or a text is a great way to know that people care and are thinking of you, sometimes physically standing next to someone means so much more. Attending that service was about expressing my genuine care and concern to Josh and the family. Supporting them, as with anyone else at the club, in the community or in my church, was not simply about offering a few well-meaning words. It was about acting on what I had said and following through on my promises.

Sometimes it is very easy to say something without really meaning it and sometimes even with no intention of following through on it. I believe that as a follower of Jesus my words should count and that when I say I'll do something then I will. Sadly, on this I fail too often, and I struggle with the frustration of not being able to do anything about the words uttered and the promises that will be left unfulfilled. It isn't that I intentionally say things to deceive – but rather that I have the right intentions and then discover other things taking over.

Being let down by people is a horrible experience, not only when it happens, but because the next time you question whether what you have heard is a genuine offer and promise or not. I have spent many hours listening to the frustrations of those who have been on the receiving end of broken promises – at the club and in the local community. I have also experienced this personally, so know exactly how it feels. The challenge then is for me to think before making promises.

Ten days after Millsy's operation, I spoke to him to see how his recuperation was going. It was going to be a long, slow recovery, but he seemed well in himself and we enjoyed a few moments catching up. This would be something we would repeat every couple of weeks or so, just to keep in touch, and when he had an appointment or check-up, I'd make sure I contacted him to see what the news was.

The evening before the home match against Barrow, Greg Reid and I welcomed a youth group from a local church to come and have a look around the club and behind the scenes, ahead of watching the game. It was an idea that emerged soon after I began my chaplaincy at the club. On average we do about three tours a season, and this month we had a group from Queen Edith Chapel coming along. In recent years we have partnered with Cambridge and District Youth for Christ as they have the local contacts, and as a result the tours have evolved. We make no charge for these, but the young people pay for their match-day tickets and so add a few numbers to the gate. It also gives them an opportunity to invite their friends along and for us to share a little about what we believe.

On this occasion, the evening started with a quiz before I took the young people on a brief tour of the hospitality area, and to the dressing room. Here the kit was all set out for the game and the young people sat while we talked about the match-day routines, gave them some general information and told stories about life as a professional footballer.

On these occasions Greg always gives a rundown of the work of the physio and shows them the kit and equipment he uses. He does occasionally strap an ankle or a head just to demonstrate how he might go about it. After this we normally head, via the referees' room, to the away dressing room where Greg and I share something of our story about being Christians. Throughout the evening we invite questions and interaction.

Each group that books in is aware that we will share something about our faith, so it isn't something we spring on them. How we do this, what we say and in what way we say it depends a little on the nature of the group, how they have responded over the evening and

what the leaders have told us about the proportion of the group that
attend church on Sundays as opposed to simply attending the youth
group.

For me, I usually share something of my journey and how
football and faith have merged in my life, but I also point out that to
me faith is more important and why that is. Football is very
temporal – it is, as I have mentioned earlier, a fickle business, but
faith in a God who does not change is truly a wonderful thing. I also
usually talk about how we can find our true value – not in the roar of
the crowd, or the player ratings in the paper, but in God.

Greg shares how he chose to follow Jesus when he was a
teenager. Here's his story in his own words.

> I grew up in what wasn't an overtly Christian household.
> My mum had a strong Christian faith. However my dad, up
> until a couple of years before he died, didn't have a faith
> and neither did either of my older brothers.
>
> Despite this, ever since I can remember, I always believed
> there was a God. I don't know why – I certainly wasn't bashed
> over the head by a family Bible! It was just something that
> seemed to be deep within me right from the start.
>
> As I grew into my teenage years, like most people of that
> age I guess, I began to consider the big questions about life
> – who are we?, how did we get here?, what are we here
> for? what happens when we die? – that type of stuff.
>
> When I was 14 my mates and I began going to a youth
> club that was put on by a local church. For a group of kids
> who were sports mad it was great, in the summer we would
> play football, cricket, tennis and so on and in the winter we
> would play table tennis, darts and pool. In addition to the
> games and sporting activities the people running the club
> took the time to get to know us individually and shared
> their faith with us in a low-key friendly manner.
>
> During one conversation where I was asked what I believed
> I responded by saying that as I believed in God and tried to
> live a good life, I thought that when I died I would go to
> heaven.

It was a shock to be told that according to God's word that wouldn't be enough to ensure my salvation. An analogy of being in an aircraft which is going to crash was used. You might look at a parachute and say, 'that will save me,' but unless you act on it and put the parachute on and then pull the rip cord, it isn't going to be of much use to you!

A few weeks later, we all attended a two-week summer camp at the coast. Again it was organised sports from morning till night, with the same low-key Christian input. It was during this time that the reality of my situation hit home and I decided to accept Jesus Christ as my Lord and Saviour.

It is a decision that I have never regretted; during all the highs and lows (more lows if I'm honest!) he has always been there with me, helping and guiding me (when I allow him to!).

During the eleven years I have been at the club I have worked for ten different managers, some good and some not so good – that is the nature of football, nothing stays the same for long. The biggest help my faith has been to me is to know that no matter how often things change at the club my future is secure through my relationship with the Lord.

Having shared our stories, we draw the evening to a close, answering any questions anyone may have, but leaving the leaders to follow up with any conversations after that. On one occasion after a tour we heard that two girls had decided that they wanted to become Christians, and were subsequently baptised, which was a tremendous encouragement. Greg and I are fully aware that we were but one part in that process, but it was definitely encouraging for us.

For the match-day experience, I ensure the group gets a mention in the match-day programme, as well as over the tannoy. They get to meet a couple of players – perhaps those injured or not involved in the game at half-time – and at the end they get a photo of the group with a couple of players. The tours have been popular and the group that weekend certainly seemed to enjoy themselves. And I know that one member of a youth group which had a tour a few seasons back ended up becoming a season ticket holder as a result of the tour. For me that is a win-win situation; a tangible benefit to the club as well as an opportunity for Greg and me to share our faith.

The Barrow match also happened to be the game we had chosen as our 'Kick It Out' match. Ahead of the game the previous week the local paper had done a photo and feature in the paper about it, and at the game we had members of the Cambridge Ethnic Community Forum handing out leaflets and 'One Game, One Community' stickers and pin badges. As the players walked out on to the pitch before kick off, the 'Kick It Out' flag was paraded in front of them.

All in all, the links had been created, the message had been put out, and it was deemed a successful venture. The game was a success too, with the U's running out 3–1 winners. The atmosphere at the end of the game was very different from that of the previous home game.

This game also saw the launch of a new book that had been written by the fans, *Cambridge 'Til I Die!* It was a project that had initially been set up as part of the centenary celebrations that are coming up in 2012/13. But the project had gathered its own momentum and had been produced early. Fans had written in with their favourite stories about following the U's and the best of these had made it into print. The official launch of the book took place before the game and then before kick-off and at half-time we gave it a plug with a handful of former U's back with us for the occasion.

Introducing talk of Jesus into a conversation with a player at the training ground is not, in my experience, something that happens very naturally! For me, though, because of what I believe, I have wrestled with how to introduce players to the Christian message in a way that is not tacky and forced but real and honest.

Christians in Sport run termly evenings at a church in Cambridge, and Graham Daniels, Executive Director of Christians in
Sport and an ex-pro at Cambridge United, often hosts these evenings. They are shaped around good food, good-quality entertainment in the form of a sports quiz and a well-delivered talk from
Graham, one of his colleagues or a Christian sportsman or woman,
past or present. The evening concludes with an opportunity to talk
further, to take literature, or to attend a further course. These
evenings attract between 100 and 200 people and are very popular
and well run.

Greg began taking one or two local players along and when I
started he invited me to join them. Over time, this has developed,
and now Jez George comes along when he can, and usually a
handful of the younger players come along too. These evenings
have proved very helpful over the years in opening up conversations
about what I believe and what some of the players believe. It also
gives me a little security in not abusing my position, something I am
very aware of. In my case, as chaplain, it allows me to leave the door
open with the players should they wish to talk further, and often
there will be a few texts back and forth following these evenings.

The October event took place and as usual Greg and I attended
with Jez and four of the young lads. It was an enjoyable evening,
meeting up with the players outside the football context is something I have always found hugely beneficial. Because the evening is
led by Christians in Sport, the Christian message is applied to life,
but always with a definite sporting perspective, recognising those
that are there are very clearly from the sporting world. These
evenings are a really helpful part of my work, and something that
over the years, I have had growing confidence in inviting players
along to.

The following Saturday saw the U's in FA Cup action with a home
draw against Lewes. Teams in the Blue Square Bet Premier League
join the competition in the fourth (and final) qualifying round. The
various cup competitions can provide a good unexpected source of
income. It is very hard to budget for a good cup run because of the
nature of the competition. Whether you are home or away you get a

percentage of the gate receipts on the day, and if you progress, you also get some money at each stage.

For this game we had arranged a collection under the Smile Scheme in memory of Josh's gran. The family had chosen a charity to benefit from gifts given in her memory – they came along to take up the collection, and we'd arranged a nice article for the match-day programme, complete with photo. The game itself went well, with the U's progressing to round one following a 3–0 win.

Towards the end of the month I was presented with another opportunity to address a group of folk about my work as chaplain. This time it was a group from Horringer Court Community Church in Bury St Edmunds. They put on a supper evening and quiz night, and I was then asked to share a little about my work. Having a little bit longer than the assembly it meant I was able to share a few more stories, as well as talking more about why I am involved as I am. The evening was well put together – for the quiz we were in teams and I was with some folk I knew from years back when I lived in Bury St Edmunds. We didn't do overly well in the quiz – maybe we were too distracted by catching up!

After the quiz and some food, I was asked to talk and for about twenty minutes or so I talked folk through how I got involved with Cambridge United and what I do as chaplain. I used some of the stories from the past few seasons to highlight various aspects of the work and then opened up the evening for questions.

Being a follower of Jesus is the most important thing in my life and I love the opportunity to tell people about this – it is one of the main reasons I do the job I do. Given the opportunity to share about chaplaincy at Cambridge United, I will always default back to why I do it – what it is that motivates me. And that is the fact that I love God and as a result of that I love people and want them to hear about how wonderful God is. But as part of that, I love to provoke people to ask questions. I'm not a typical Baptist minister – often when players come to the club and I introduce myself they look quizzically at me as if I'm pulling a fast one as I don't fit their image of what a 'vicar' or 'rev' looks like.

Through the medium of football, and in particular the little piece of that I experience, it is my hope that as I share my story, people may start to search and ask questions, to reconcile the message they are hearing with the messenger delivering it, and to think about a God who somehow doesn't quite fit in the box they had made for him. And as they begin to allow God out of that box, he will begin to show them exactly who he is and how wonderful he is.

What I didn't know about that evening was there was a Brechin City fan present who was so struck by what he'd heard that he wrote an article for the Brechin City programme for their game against Forfar Athletic. It just reminded me that you can never be sure how far words will travel, and while that is great when it is good news, it challenges us to think about the negative things we can say – once the words are out there, we have no control over them!

The month ended with another overnighter – this time the U's travelled to Gateshead and turned in a decent performance to record another game undefeated with a 3–2 win. This meant that they finished the month lying in 14th place with a record of played 17, won 5, drawn 5, lost 7.

As has been mentioned previously, things change quickly in football. The month had started pretty disastrously, with two losses to two teams we were expected to beat in Bath City and Hayes & Yeading, and amidst calls for the manager to be ousted, hope of a 'successful' season seemed to be ebbing away. But by the end of the month we had back-to-back wins. For many around the club – management, players and supporters – the turning point in the month had been the hard-fought point earned at Fleetwood in front of the TV cameras. It certainly appeared to have changed the course of the month for the U's. Just how long the U's would continue in this form remained to be seen.

We had also been handed a home tie in the first round of the FA Cup against League One highflyers Huddersfield Town, who at the time of the draw were second to Brighton. Not only that, but the game had been chosen to be screened live, meaning a 5.15 p.m. kick-off and, more importantly for the club, a bit of extra and unplanned for cash. With the bit of form the U's were beginning to show, confidence was high that we might, at our place, be able to get something from the game.

Only time would tell – and there was only a week to wait!

October Results

Sat 2	Blue Square Bet Premier	**United 1 Bath City 2** *Russell*
Tues 5	Blue Square Bet Premier	**Hayes & Yeading 2 United 0**
Sun 10	Blue Square Bet Premier	**Fleetwood Town 2 United 2** *Stavrinou, Willmott (pen)*
Sat 16	Blue Square Bet Premier	**United 3 Barrow 1** *Russell, o.g., Coulson*
Sat 23	FA Cup 4th qualifying round	**United 3 Lewes 0** *Gray, Wright, Russell*
Sat 30	Blue Square Bet Premier	**Gateshead 2 United 3** *Coulson, Gray, Russell*

November 2010

The local media have become increasingly aware of my role at the club, and from time to time the request comes for a quote, or more usually to do a radio interview on a particular subject.

Jeremy Sallis, the breakfast show presenter for Radio Cambridgeshire, made contact with me about the scattering of ashes on the pitch at Cambridge United. This was as a result of a visit he had made to the local firework factory in the build-up to 5 November, where he had been told that they receive many requests from relatives asking for ashes to be put into rockets.

When I began my work as chaplain back in 2005, the stadium officer, Ian Darler, had said to me at the time that there were two things he could immediately think of that I could help him with. The first was when he is asked to scatter ashes on the pitch – he usually gets a couple of requests a season – and the second was the occasional situation when a supporter collapses. While the paramedics are doing their job, the stewards can often see and experience things that they could do with talking to someone about.

As it happens, since August 2005, Ian had only had two requests for the scattering of ashes – the first was when I was on holiday, and on the second occasion the family wanted a very small and simple affair.

So I suggested to Jeremy Sallis that Ian Darler, not me, was the man he should interview, but despite trying to side-step the need to be in the studio early in the morning, Jeremy insisted that he would like me there as well.

Ian did a great interview, telling some of the stories of where the ashes were scattered, and some of the more unusual requests he had received. My contribution was to say that I hadn't done any yet!

That afternoon, I had a call from Ian. A lady had turned up at the club asking if the club allowed the scattering of ashes on the pitch – it was her granddad that had passed away, and he had been an avid United fan. This was unconnected to the radio interview, but Ian had advised her that it was permitted and he would contact me to officiate. We left it with them to get back to us in due course.

It reminded me again of the incredible privilege clergy have in being invited in to help families to mark the most significant moments in life; births, weddings and deaths. Not working in a parish context, perhaps I have fewer opportunities than other ministers to do this. But there have been some wonderful opportunities within the work at the club to share in these times. As someone who has some experience in handling such matters, there have been occasions when I have been asked by the club to contact a family – 'You'll know what to say', I'm told.

The other thing I do from time to time is visit hospitals. Some people have a real aversion to hospitals – my dad for one! Fortunately, I think I take after my mum in this regard (she is a retired nurse), and hospitals do not faze me, so I feel very comfortable visiting people in hospital whoever and whatever the situation.

During November I ended up making regular visits to Addenbrooke's Hospital. It began when Blaine Hudson, one of the younger players in the squad, spun his car off the road on a wet night heading back to Cambridge from home as he avoided a deer that had stepped out in front of him. The car had flipped over and ended up on the embankment. Blaine had only just filled the car up with fuel and he was concerned about it going up in flames, so he'd punched his way out of the back windscreen as the door was jammed.

Fortunately for Blaine his injuries weren't life-threatening, nor were they career-threatening. He needed surgery to his hands to repair the nasty gashes caused by punching through the rear windscreen, and an operation to repair his shoulder which had been dislocated and had torn ligaments.

Visiting him on that first occasion, it was clear that the incident had left him shaken. He recognised just how fortunate he had been. He had been on the receiving end of an unfortunate accident, through no fault of his own. I was also able to meet his mum and grandma, and over the ensuing weeks kept in contact with them and checked on his progress. Blaine lives in Norfolk, but all his treatment and surgery took place in Cambridge, so the journey down the A11 became a regular trip for him and I used to try to take the opportunity to meet him for a coffee in the hospital concourse following his appointments.

During this time there were moments when he was quite reflective and times when he was low, as progress didn't appear to be as swift as he would like, but there was always a willingness to talk. He certainly was one who missed being around the other lads, being active and training.

And that has been true for many a player who faces a lengthy rehabilitation. There are times when they need to rest, and they can become highly frustrating times for men who have been so used to being so active. And then when things don't appear to be going as fast as they would like, they can easily become despondent. Keeping in touch, helping them to try and keep some perspective is important. In the case of Blaine, to be able to remind him of how fortunate he had been to still have a career, and even a life, after what had happened was a blessing, and a few weeks' discomfort and frustration were not much to have to endure in the grand scheme of things.

But then isn't that true for all of us? Don't we all have that tendency to allow things to overwhelm us? At times like that, having people that will help us refocus and keep things in perspective is important.

So Blaine joined Adam Miller on the long-term injured list – Blaine would be out for about four months, while Millsy was not likely to be back before pre-season 2011. Adam Marriott was still out with an ankle injury picked up away at Hayes & Yeading, and Luke Berry and Daryl Coakley, two more of the young lads, were also still out injured.

Also on the injured list was Brian Saah, who needed a double hernia operation and went under the surgeon's knife at the start of the month. For Greg as physio he needs to make a judgement call with players in this kind of situation. Some operations can be postponed until the end of the season as with necessary treatment, rest and painkillers, players can play through till then. In Brian's case he was struggling with each game, and the decision was taken to move ahead with surgery in the hope that he would be back in contention in time for the Christmas period when games come thick and fast. Because it was a double hernia, Brian was at home for the first couple of weeks resting, so text messaging was a way to keep in touch and send him greetings.

A further blow came when Daryl Clare broke his finger badly in a freak training ground clash. Although fortunately not requiring surgery, it would mean he would not be available for a few weeks. Martin Ling's bad fortune with injuries to key players seemed to be continuing. And that, combined with players beginning to pick up suspensions, meant that the squad was starting to look a little thin.

The next United game was the first round FA Cup match, live on ESPN, against Huddersfield Town. There was a really good atmosphere in the stadium, with a buzz of excitement and anticipation. Paul Carden, who had been struggling with a back complaint, was declared fit to take his place in central midfield. In the FA Cup, teams are allowed to name up to seven substitutes, and with the squad decimated by injury, Martin Ling was forced to name three youth team players on the bench, one of whom, James Brighton, made his first step into the first team squad. The pundits, including ex-United legend Dion Dublin, were there, along with the Trophy, set up in a makeshift studio in the corner of the ground.

As an announcer, live games are always a little bit different; you're never quite sure when making announcements whether you are cutting across anyone on the TV! The timing of the players coming out of the tunnel is dictated not by the referee but by the TV crew when they're switching back from the commercials. And there are cameras in the dressing rooms and cables running everywhere. It is always a little bit surreal, and the TV crews never talk to you and make sure you know what they are doing, or let you know if they want you to do anything.

The game proved to be a very entertaining 0–0 draw. Both teams had the chances to snatch the win, but United had upped their game to compete with the League One high-flyers. So it was to be a replay, ten days on in Huddersfield. The lads could rightly be proud of themselves, if perhaps ruing the chances that they had missed. They could certainly take confidence from that game though. And it was another game unbeaten.

To be honest, I am very fortunate as a chaplain. My presence around the club, around the ground or the training facilities is not questioned and the way I am treated is very humbling, because I am accepted. This was demonstrated at the training ground following the FA Cup match, when I was able to be part of a meeting Jez and Nolan had with the scholars. The first team were having a cooling-down session at the gym as they had another game midweek. But the scholars were in as usual, and following training and lunch, over a coffee, the meeting tackled a number of practical issues.

Jez and Nolan work hard with the scholars on the training ground to improve their game and give them every opportunity to make the step up to a professional contract. But they equally give time to ensuring the lads learn discipline, appreciate the privilege they have in being part of the team, and think about how they relate to one another – how their actions impact upon others. There were a couple of issues to address on this occasion.

Firstly, three of the London academy lads were being brought in as scholars as some of the more advanced second years were in and around the first team squad and numbers within the youth development squad were tight. These lads were moving into the digs and so there needed to be a reorganisation of the houses and who was sharing with whom. Rather than Jez and Nolan telling the lads how it should be, they helped guide the scholars in working it out for themselves, asking leading questions and provoking them to think about the impact each scenario would have, whose temperaments would work best together and who would clash. It was fascinating to be a 'fly on the wall' for that conversation.

The scholars had also been set the task of organising a fundraising event, and had been put into three teams to plan and deliver their particular event. Listening in and observing how the lads interacted – who the dominant voices were, and who had the insightful and helpful voices – was certainly enlightening, and some of the challenges that Jez had spoken to me about over the weeks became obvious. But for me, the fact that my presence was just accepted as normal was very humbling and I felt privileged to be there.

For our midweek game we locked horns for the first time with one of the two recently relegated teams from League Two, Grimsby

Town. This ended in a 1–1 draw, so we had another game unbeaten. However, events on the pitch were somewhat overshadowed by events off it on this particular occasion.

Having just finished announcing the teams before kick-off, I received a call from Ian Darler to tell me that one of the fans had collapsed and the paramedics were working on him. I was asked to go up to the stand and be available to the stewards. When I arrived at the top of the main stand, the paramedics, St John's Ambulance team and club doctors were working on a man lying flat on the walkway. I stood nearby and, to be honest, I just prayed. I had no idea who it was, or what was happening. But I prayed that God would help the medics, and that he would be with this fan, whoever he was. I stood near one of the stewards who had been nearby when he had first been found. Natalie also kept me informed regarding the arrival of the ambulance as she had the earpiece and was in radio contact with Ian Darler.

After about half an hour the man was loaded onto a stretcher and carried down and put into the ambulance. I spoke to one of the police officers and obtained the man's name and his wife's contact details.

At half time, I did my usual announcements on the pitch, and then headed back to the control tower. Here I found the steward who had been first on the scene, Alan Millard, sitting drinking a cup of tea. A few years previously I had had the privilege of leading the funeral service for Alan's father – Alan had found him dead, and the experience that evening had caused him to relive those moments when he found his father. I was able to sit with Alan for a few minutes while he drank his tea and talk to him about what he had seen and what had then happened. When Alan was feeling strong enough to go back on duty, I headed over to see Natalie, and like Alan she was feeling a little stronger.

Following the conclusion of the game, I headed up to Addenbrooke's to see if I could locate the fan, whose name was Paul, and his family. After about half an hour, I was able to find his wife in the family room. At this point she hadn't seen her husband. I was able to talk through as best as I could what had happened that evening. Paul had sat in his chair, and just before kick-off had had a heart attack. Alan and one or two sitting nearby had managed to get him to the back of the stand where he was laid down and treatment began. By the time the paramedics had got to him he had no pulse, but they were able to shock him and get his heart working again. Things were still very critical, but Paul was stable. I left his wife Lynn with my details and promised to ring the next day.

I kept in touch with Lynn and Paul over the following days, passing on regular updates to Ian, Alan and one of the fans who had been sitting nearby. I was able to pop in to see Paul on a couple of occasions, but each time I went in he was being checked over or moved. However, eventually after a few days, I found him sitting up in bed and was able to meet Paul properly and answer some of his questions.

We arranged for his wife and two sons to come to the game against Tamworth as they wanted to thank those involved in person. It was perhaps a slightly awkward moment, especially for the medics – it isn't often their experience to be thanked for what they have done in such a personal way. They very much appreciated Lynn taking the time to visit, but as they said to me afterwards, they were just doing their job and didn't quite know what to say to her! The stewards also appreciated the contact and were pleased to hear of Paul's progress. Paul had his instructions to rest and football was off the menu for a few weeks until the weather improved and he was given the OK.

The reality is that 99 per cent of the fans who were at the ground that night would not have had a clue what was going on. The stewards and the medics did a thoroughly professional job, and there was no panic. Ian told me this was the second occasion this had happened at the club, and on both occasions, they had managed to resuscitate the fans. Again, I felt incredibly privileged to support the family and stewards through this time.

One of the things that I have been working on with Ian Darler over the years has been the idea of establishing a Book of Remembrance at the club. As has been mentioned, there are a number of folk whose ashes are scattered on the pitch. There are also many other fans who are perhaps buried elsewhere, but whose families would like them to be remembered in this way.

Over recent seasons we had looked at various alternatives. A suitable site for a memorial stone was identified, and beginning a Book of Remembrance seemed the logical next step. A number of fans had paid some money towards some paving, but this had never been done, and after a few years, it was decided to use the money to create a memorial garden, with a wall created from the dedications and entries submitted.

I was tasked to create the wording for the memorial stone and to source the Book of Remembrance, with the plan to have it established and opened on the day of the Carol Service.

As chaplain, I try to help the club to think through how it can help fans and players to mark these significant life moments. For some supporters the football club has been their life, but how can we help their families remember that? And should the ground be redeveloped and the club relocate, how can we ensure that the memories of these folk are not dishonoured in that move?

It seems to me that people are still looking for those sacred spaces, those places of remembering. In years gone by, families may have found this place in a church or at the graveside. Today, it seems that those places are elsewhere – football stadiums, the roadside, public spaces or the school gates – significant locations other than the church or cemetery. In that context, how can we ensure that Cambridge United Football Club is set up and prepared for this? And as a minister of a church just up the road, what does this say to me about what our church is like? Are there lessons we need to learn? Are there different ways we need to work and minster? Because people still want a place to go – they just don't think of church as being that place as they once used to.

I was very pleased to be invited to a meeting at the club to discuss a new 'Kick It Out' initiative, this time with a particular focus on sexual orientation. At the meeting was Miriam Lynn from the Cambridge charity SexYOUality, which works with Lesbian, Gay and Bisexual young people. I've known Miriam for a few years as she was a ward councillor for the Abbey ward when I first started at Barnwell Baptist Church. Miriam is involved in putting together a programme of events in the city each February to mark LGBT

Month. The theme of sport had been chosen for these events for 2011 and 2012, and this had led to conversations with Cambridge United. We discussed plans to run another 'Kick It Out' day at a game in February, at which the LGBT team would be invited to hand out literature to the crowd. Nick Parker again agreed to pull it together, and it was good for me to be able to support him in that role.

I have always been committed to the idea that, as chaplain to the football club, I am not just representing myself, or even Barnwell Baptist Church. In many ways, I am a representative of all the churches of Cambridge and beyond – how I behave and act will have an effect on how people at the club perceive the Church. I have also been keen from the outset that in some way the churches will feel some connection with the work I do, rather than it being perceived as Stuart Wood doing his own thing.

So when I first started my work as chaplain at Cambridge United, as well as linking up with SCORE, I also became an associate chaplain with Chaplaincy to People at Work, a Cambridge-based organisation seeking to provide workplace chaplaincy. This is an interdenominational organisation, and through the lead chaplain, part-time chaplain and a team of associate chaplains it works in business, retail, education, the public sector and of course, sport across Cambridgeshire and Huntingdonshire. I have found this group to be a very helpful support to my work locally, and it promotes wider recognition of the role. As chaplains we meet every couple of months or so to share stories and prayer requests and look at how our respective chaplaincies are developing.

Personally, I don't have any problem relating to people who hold different views to my own – whether that is in regard to the Christian faith, my views on moral or ethical issues or whether football is the best sport ever! But neither am I ignorant of the challenges these differing views sometimes create. I know that there is a very broad spectrum of beliefs and theological viewpoints on homosexuality among church leaders, both locally and nationally, and it was possible that some of the people I related to locally might have been uncomfortable with my support for and involvement with the LGBT initiative. I was very conscious that it would be very easy to be misunderstood or misrepresented.

However, I believe that part of my role as chaplain is to help Cambridge United Football Club to be accessible to everyone, and that includes those whose sexual orientation is different to mine, just as it includes those whose faith is different from mine. Should I not make the Muslim football fan feel welcome? Of course! The football club is a place where anyone should be able to come and feel welcome, regardless of their religious beliefs, gender, sexual orientation, age, race or disability – the six areas the 'Kick It Out' campaign seeks to address. My working to make the club accessible to everyone by supporting the club's participation in the 'Kick It Out' campaign is simply about making people feel welcome at Cambridge United, especially those who have in the past been made to feel unwelcome or even threatened.

The next game was an away fixture at Kettering Town – the U's took a first half lead thanks to two goals by Robbie Willmott, before Kettering got themselves back into it in the second half. The game ended in a 2–2 draw, and although this was another game unbeaten, a run that now extended to seven games, it was perhaps a case of two more dropped points rather than a point gained.

This was followed by the replay of the FA Cup first round match, a game that with my working schedules I was able to travel to, albeit by rearranging a meeting. So I jumped on the team coach and headed north.

I have been very thankful for Martin Ling's openness to me being around and his acceptance of me in my role. Being around the players for the pre-match meal and being in the dressing room during pre-match team talk and as they prepared for the match is a real privilege. On this occasion, although I was invited by Martin to sit in the dugout, I opted to sit with the staff in the stands.

The U's played a fantastic match, taking the lead through Rory McAuley. Heading into the final moments Huddersfield threw everything at United and snatched an equaliser at the death. Just as the game appeared to be heading for extra time, Huddersfield grabbed the winner deep into added time. It was heartbreaking, and yet the players could walk off with heads held high – they had achieved more than most had predicted and had come close to what would have been a remarkable victory.

With the Youth and Community Trust still in its infancy, it was proving to be an interesting journey seeing how the Trust fitted in with the overall work of the football club. With its formation, there had become three main entities promoting the work of Cambridge United – the club itself, which includes the players and staff, along with the brand; the Cambridge Fans United Trust, which is the supporters' trust; and the Youth and Community Trust, which seeks to provide a structure to deliver the club's work for children and young people right across the region. It was estimated that by the end of the first year, the Trust would have had contact with around 10,000 children and young people across the region through schools, after-school clubs, and community events as well as running holiday courses and specific coaching courses.

Talking to Nigel Ashman about his role and how he saw it developing was really helpful for me in getting a handle on where areas of overlap could be and also where the gaps were.

As the season went on, I found myself increasingly involved in linking the various elements together. Perhaps I, more than anyone else, was able to move between the three entities without prejudice – it hasn't been my experience yet that I am viewed with suspicion by any of those groups. In fact, some of the groups were looking to me to be more pro-active in linking them together. So I will no doubt continue to be involved in working across the different entities that together make Cambridge United the unique club that it is.

In spite of the fact that these groups had their own agendas, there was a realisation that they were all ultimately after the same thing – the success of Cambridge United Football Club. It is one of the similarities in some ways between the Church and football that I see – the 90 minutes on a Saturday afternoon or Sunday morning sets the tone for everything else. From a footballing perspective, having a successful team on the pitch makes the club easier to sell commercially; it raises the profile amongst young people joining coaching courses; the community is more willing to want to be associated with it; and the number of fans that turn up on match days will increase. From a church perspective having a 'successful' service on Sunday mornings means that more people will start to come (and come back); it provides a springboard for work in the community and people are more willing to put their money in the offering plate.

Our next match was at home against Tamworth. Before this, Greg and I welcomed a group of men from St Andrew's the Great on a tour, as we had done last month for the youth group. This was only the second time we had done this with a men's group as opposed to a youth group, and after the tour, we headed out for a curry at the Pipasha Indian Restaurant directly opposite the club. It was fascinating to see that some of these men were as excited as some of the young people at seeing behind the scenes.

At the Tamworth game, the Mayor of Cambridge was present and what a game she witnessed! Before kick-off we held a minute's silence to remember a former assistant manager, Paddy Sowden, who had died, and also to acknowledge Remembrance Day, which had not been marked because of a slip-up the previous week at Kettering Town.

From when I first started as chaplain, it has been my privilege to be asked to introduce a minute's silence or applause. At the beginning of my time, there was someone else who read out the teams and did the pitchside announcements, but whenever there was a minute's silence he would hand the microphone over to me. I have never known a minute's silence to be spoiled at United; they have always been impeccably observed. There have been some very poignant moments as we've invited the families of those we're remembering to come and stand pitchside with me for those moments. I feel incredibly privileged to be there and to share in those very special moments. Although there are over two thousand fans joining in, it does at times seem to be a strangely personal and intimate moment as well.

Along with the Mayor of Cambridge, we also welcomed Pudsey Bear to the ground for the Tamworth game, collecting on behalf of BBC Children in Need as part of our Smile Scheme.

The game itself seemed to be a bit of a disaster, with United trailing 2–0 at half time, this becoming 3–0 early in the second half. However, with the introduction of Jordan Patrick and Adam Marriott the game was turned on its head. Robbie Willmott scored from a fortuitous penalty, JP scored a second and then Adam Marriott produced an audacious chip from fully 20 yards to level the game. Despite the momentum being with the U's, they couldn't quite find the fourth and the match ended 3–3, but under the circumstances it certainly felt as if we had gained more than a point.

Following on from the minute's silence held at the Tamworth game for former assistant manager Paddy Sowden, I attended his funeral. Paddy had been manager Ron Atkinson's assistant in the early seventies, and had also served as first team coach. There have been a few occasions when I have attended funerals of former players, fans or staff as a representative of the club, in most cases for people that I have never met personally. In the early days it was something that I was occasionally asked if I would do, and I was willing to oblige. Latterly, it is something that I have tended to offer as part of my work and service of the club.

Again, I reflect with gratitude on the club that I serve as chaplain. I am aware that what I do, and the opportunities I have are not possible at bigger clubs. Even at Cambridge United it isn't possible to attend the funerals of all the fans who pass away, and indeed I often don't hear about them until after the event.

At the funeral, I sat next to Lance Key, the goalkeeping coach at Rushden & Diamonds. I had got to know Lance when he was the goalkeeper at Histon Football Club, and he had run a coaching course that my son Curtis had attended. Over the years, I had enjoyed the usual amount of banter with him, and had always found him very personable. It was good to catch up with him, and in doing so to talk about the situation at Rushden, where Canon Roger Knight has been the chaplain for a number of years. After that conversation I was able to swap emails with Roger, which would prove helpful in the weeks that were to come.

Next up for the U's was another home game against the struggling Altrincham. The previous manager had parted company with the club earlier in the season, and the new management team were known to me from my time at United. Ken McKenna had been the chief scout in Gary Brabin's time as manager, and Ken's assistant, Stuart Bimson, was both a former player at United (before my time) and with Gary Brabin had been first team coach. In their squad they also had Mark Beesley, another ex-United player, who made his debut for Altrincham that afternoon when he came on as a second half substitute. It was good to catch up with them all.

Also featuring in the Altrincham side were ex-U's Marc Joseph and Matt Somner, both of whom had left before I arrived as chaplain. I had hoped the Altrincham chaplain, Andy Barclay-Watt, would have been able to travel down, but in the end it wasn't possible so we had to resort to swapping emails.

The game itself in the end proved a comfortable one for United, with both strikers scoring two goals, one in each half. Danny Naisbitt saved a penalty at the end to preserve a clean sheet, resulting in a 4–0 win. Ian and the team had worked hard to get the pitch ready for the game, and at the end Ken McKenna said he couldn't wait to get back up to Altrincham because it was warm up there!

Cambridge United was formed in 1912 – the first recorded game was in the summer of 1912. So a couple of seasons previously, conversations had started about the upcoming centenary season. There had been some meetings arranged, none of which I had been able to attend, although I was very pleased to be considered as being able to contribute to the conversation and discussion. However, I had used the SCORE chaplains' network to find what other clubs had done to mark significant anniversaries, and had received a couple of interesting responses which I had fed in to the group.

I finally managed to make a meeting. It had been decided that as the first game was in July 1912, the centenary could have been marked in either the 2011/12 or the 2012/13 season, but in view of the plan to produce a special centenary kit, to fall in with the current kit cycle, the celebrations would be during the 2012/13 season. I had suggested holding a centenary service, and although many of those gathered round the table would not have counted themselves 'religious', this was well received.

When I first started back in 2005, one of the first things that I arranged was a carol service at the ground on an evening before Christmas. It was important to me that it didn't cost the club any money to put it on, as I didn't want the service not to happen for financial reasons. So I was able to find three local companies to help support this event – Ridgeons, Coulsons, and The David Ball group. Their sponsorship, together with funds from Barnwell Baptist Church, Hope Cambridge and St Andrew's Street Baptist Church for the first year, enabled the event to go ahead each year with no cost to the club.

The carol service also needed to be accessible to the local community – making it an event that people would wander along to was important – so we made it very traditional, choosing carols people liked to sing, rather than introducing ones they were less familiar with. And we aimed, in a very low-key way, to challenge folk to think about the real meaning of Christmas.

We had held four successful events from 2005–8, with involvement from the local media, local schools, the club and local residents. But the 2009 event had been cancelled due to the snow. So it was with a sense of trepidation that I began putting in place the necessary arrangements for the Cambridge United Carols at the Abbey 2010. This was to be the first year that I had spoken at it myself – I had always up to this point played host. And this year I scaled back the plans; rather than shipping in PA equipment, I planned to use the club's tannoy system.

In 2009, Martin Ling had arranged for the whole squad to be at the event for the first time, although in the end the event had had to be cancelled. Before then it had been the one or two local players that had been asked to attend. However, with the plans for 2010 this wasn't going to be possible because the players' Christmas party clashed and they were away. I had the local radio station involved (Jeremy Sallis was going to be one of our readers), the publicity was complete; all was in place – I just needed the weather to be good. And then the snow arrived! Our next scheduled game against Rushden & Diamonds away at the end of the month was the first of a number of fixtures to fall foul of the cold snap. Would Carols at the Abbey 2010 survive?

The month ended with United lying in 13th place with a record of played 21, won 6, drawn 8, lost 7. The unbeaten league run extended back to the beginning of October, the last defeat being to Hayes & Yeading. And in that period they had pushed Huddersfield hard, narrowly missing out on a second round FA Cup match at home to either Macclesfield or Southend. One or two of the players were starting to come back into contention – Adam Marriott was back playing, and with some of the other players looking set to return, it would be interesting to see if United could push on from here and keep the run going.

November Results

Sat 6	FA Cup 1st round	**United 0 Huddersfield Town 0**
Tues 9	Blue Square Bet Premier	**United 1 Grimsby Town 1**
		Wright
Sat 13	Blue Square Bet Premier	**Kettering Town 2 United 2**
		Willmott 2
Tues 16	FA Cup 1st round (replay)	**Huddersfield Town 2 United 1**
		McAuley
Sat 20	Blue Square Bet Premier	**United 3 Tamworth 3**
		Willmott (pen), Patrick, Marriott
Sat 27	Blue Square Bet Premier	**United 4 Altrincham 0**
		Wright 2, Gray 2
Tues 30	Blue Square Bet Premier	**Rushden & Diamonds P United P**

December 2010

The next game for the U's was the away trip to Newport County, which due to TV schedules had been moved from the Saturday to the Sunday, with a 1.00 p.m. kick-off. This was the second away game to have been moved due to TV coverage – the first, the away game at Fleetwood, had been televised, while the Newport game was moved due to their previous game having been moved from the Tuesday to the Thursday so it could be televised live.

TV coverage has become such an integral part of the game now that clubs budget for TV revenue. So when ITV Digital went into administration back in 2002, many lower league clubs struggled financially as they had banked on the additional revenue that they were due from the deal struck between ITV Digital and the Football League.

But the knock-on effect of the TV cameras and the TV revenue that comes into the clubs is that games get pushed around. At Cambridge United we're only talking about a small number of games each season where this happens, but some of the top teams end up with a surprisingly small number of unaffected games. For example, for the traditional 'big four' – Manchester United, Liverpool, Chelsea and Arsenal – the number of home league games that kick off on a Saturday afternoon at 3.00 p.m. is relatively small. For some chaplains having so many Sunday afternoon games is a real issue. In Rugby Union, some Premiership clubs play most of their home games on a Sunday afternoon, due in the main to ground shares with Football League clubs.

It is one of the frustrations that we need to learn to live with in the ever-changing world of sport, because the truth is that clubs need the money the TV cameras bring in. And rather than react against it, perhaps we need to look at how we can embrace it – does it actually present any opportunities, for example? At Wasps Rugby Union club, the chaplain, Rev. David Chawner, will often host a short service before Sunday games for stewards, staff and fans, as for many of them match-day responsibilities make attending their own church service impossible.

Having geared ourselves up for the trek west, the Newport game was called off – a frozen pitch was to blame.

As was becoming apparent through the season, my role at the club had attracted and created opportunities to develop community links. Another had started to emerge through November, as I was contacted about an event in Cambridge, the Cambridge Homeless World Cup. Organised by one of the local Rotary clubs, the first tournament had been held in May 2010; it included a number of teams from the different charities working with the homeless in Cambridge, from the Night Shelter to the YMCA, and also featured a police team. Interestingly, Musa Kamara, the captain of the winning YMCA team, who was also chosen as the player of the tournament, went on to represent England at the Homeless World Cup in Rio de Janeiro, Brazil, where he captained the England team to reach the quarter-finals.

The event had been so successful that there were plans to hold it again in May 2011. Through Simon Oliver, a local Methodist minister, I was contacted to see if and how the club might be able to get involved, and so Simon and I arranged a meeting with Mike Smith, the local organiser, and Nigel Ashman from the Youth and Community Trust to talk about the event and to see how we could help. It proved a useful meeting, and we all went away to work out how we could link the club to the event.

As chaplain, my role has been to open doors to these projects, rather than delivering them, and regular contact with Nigel Ashman to see how opportunities that were emerging tied in with his work was becoming increasingly important.

And as with so many things finance was the key. The trust needed to raise significant money year by year to keep the youth structure in place and to enable the schools and community aspects of the work to continue too. The trust's involvement with the Homeless World Cup tournament would ultimately come down to finances, and if it were successful in attracting some funding, it would be able to offer coaching to the teams and a presence on the day itself. I felt confident that due to the nature of the work, I had a source who would help finance this project.

Blaine Hudson's treatment and assessment was continuing and I caught up with him again during the month on one of his visits to Addenbrooke's Hospital. He was continuing to regain movement in his arm, although from his perspective not as quickly as he wanted to. But as Christmas passed and the month and year came to an end, he was given the all clear to begin to work with Greg Reid. Initially this would be cardio-vascular work – cycling and swimming, with some gentle exercises – until the all-clear was given on his shoulder and he could resume more strenuous impact work.

Over the years to see how players respond to treatment has been insightful – but then players are no different to us really. Some of us make good patients and others don't, and the same is true with the players. Some are very responsive and diligent in their exercises and treatment, while others are less so, either not doing their exercises properly and trying to cut corners, or pushing on too hard and risking further breakdown. Greg is vastly experienced in very quickly assessing the kind of patient the player will be, and will tend to accommodate their foibles in his treatment of them.

Our next home game was the first round of the FA Trophy. This competition is the Conference equivalent of the League Cup, being only for teams up to the Conference Premier level, and while for some teams it is not a huge priority, it does attract a Wembley final.

Our opponents were Forest Green Rovers, and we were fortunate to be drawn at home. It is one of the peculiarities of the Conference that each season there will be a couple of teams that you play home and away quite early in the season and other teams that you don't play at all until towards the end of the season. This season Forest Green were one of the teams we were playing much later – our first scheduled league fixture with them was the home game with them on 26 March, followed by an away fixture on 16 April, the season finishing on 30 April.

So having got through to December, this was to be the first time we met this team from Gloucestershire this season. They had narrowly avoided relegation the previous season; although finishing in the relegation zone, the demise of Salisbury City meant they dropped out and Forest Green were given a reprieve to remain in the Blue Square Bet Premier.

The game was on, despite the weather. Ian Darler and Mick Brown do an incredible job with the stadium and pitch, and Cambridge United can boast one of the best playing surfaces in the Conference. The 2010/11 season marked Ian's 30th year at the club, and over that time he has built up a fantastic network of volunteers and some really useful links, and is able to maintain the playing surface on a very limited budget, but not without a lot of hard work from him and his team.

One of the features of the club that I began to appreciate very early on as I talked to the staff and observed their work was that staff members like Ian, Mick, Greg and Jez are not only excellent at what they do, but also have a great deal of favour with others locally, and have some extremely useful contacts. This enables the club to have excellent access to the medical profession through Greg's contacts; to have excellent service from Ian's contacts regarding the stadium and pitch, and in Jez's case to be able to attract a high calibre of young talent. On many occasions each season these contacts are used to the benefit of the football club; something that at times can be so easily overlooked, and even undervalued.

In the end United ran out winners, progressing to the second round with a 2–1 victory, although they left it late, an own goal in injury time giving the U's the victory and entry into the second round draw. The first goal was a collector's item – a goal by Dave Partridge.

On more than one occasion since I started, there has been a tragic accident that has claimed the life of a young Cambridge United fan. December 2010 proved to be another such time. I took a phone call from Will Jones, the club's PR, media and marketing manager, about a lad who had been involved in a car accident and tragically lost his life. Harry Williams was a talented goalkeeper, playing for St Ives Town Under-18s, but was also a keen Cambridge United fan. He had been in a car with his brother and two friends when the car had left the road and hit a tree. Two of the four occupants had been killed instantly; the other two had survived although taken to hospital with serious injuries.

As has been the case on each occasion, there were calls by fans for a minute's silence, or in Harry's case a minute's applause. Following the tragedy, I was privileged to be able to arrange this with the family. I also attended the funeral, which took place on Christmas Eve at the parish church in St Ives. The church was packed with young people, family and friends, and for later arrivals there was standing room only.

As I have mentioned previously, there are times when I have attended the funeral of former players, staff and fans – people that I have never met. I do this as a mark of respect, to offer the family the club's support and condolences, to empathise with others from the club who are in mourning, and in my case to take the opportunity to pray for family and friends. This is one of the things I have sought to embrace in my ministry generally, so with each funeral I take, I try to make it as personal as I can, even when I have never met the person. It would be all too easy to simply 'do the job' but I hope and pray that I never treat anyone in that way.

And the same is true when meeting relatives at the ground for a few moments as they stand with me pitchside. As I introduce that poignant moment of silence or applause, I seek to give the best I can, to make it as personal as I can, and if that means attending a funeral to enable that to happen, then so be it.

When I look at the life and ministry of Jesus, and read how he engaged with individuals on his travels, I see a man who gave of himself to individuals. He never simply went through the motions, he always gave them his best (albeit at times and in ways that they didn't understand at the time). He valued each individual and each encounter and meeting was significant.

So, in my ministry, I receive that challenge – am I someone who will give my best in each situation, or do I at times simply go through the motions? And at Barnwell Baptist Church, are we a church that always seeks to give of our best to those who come along, or do we simply settle for 'making do'? Do individuals that come along feel valued and accepted? These are real challenges for me – not just at Barnwell, and in my role as chaplain and a minister, but in my daily life too, as I engage with neighbours and friends.

As Christmas approaches, the players traditionally visit the children's wards at Addenbrooke's Hospital and take the children presents or goody bags. In my early years at the club the visit was arranged via the club offices and I was invited to attend along with the players. In 2008 the visit had had to be cancelled at the last minute because of the winter vomiting bug and ward closures. A year later, with new staff in the club offices, I was asked to arrange the visit, having been on them previously and knowing who to make the arrangements with. Unfortunately, having put everything in place, the visit was cancelled again for the same reasons.

So in 2010 I made contact early and discovered the wards were still open. We quickly arranged with the children's play workers for the squad to visit one afternoon after training. We were able to give away to each child a calendar which the players signed as they went around the wards.

The players visited the paediatric intensive care unit and the teenage cancer ward and treatment area, as well as the other three general wards. Marvin the Moose, the club mascot, was around as well, and it was great to see smiles on the faces of many of the children and their parents and siblings.

This visit again opened up the opportunity for contact with the play team and a chance to remind them of my role. As a club, we don't want to fall into the trap of thinking we can simply turn up once a year to be seen to be doing something. We genuinely want to be available throughout the year should that be appropriate.

In the light of the cancelled visits, we spoke about the potential of a second visit each year in the summer when the players are in pre-season. For these children, while being in hospital at any time of the year is not great, being in over Christmas and over the summer holidays are particularly tough times, and so it was left that when the players returned for pre-season, the play team and I would get in touch and see what we could arrange.

I have found that being around the players when they are visiting the children provides a different insight into their temperament and personalities. Being faced with sick children – some very sick, a few terminally so – is very sobering for the players and hopefully reminds them of the incredible privilege they have of being professional footballers. There have been times when players have openly admitted to struggling with what they have seen and it has provided an opportunity for me to talk this through with them. It has also opened up conversation about my work outside of the club.

Both Martin Ling and Jez George are very committed to the players and scholars being available to give back to the community in these ways, and if they can accommodate the players being involved they are more than willing to do so. For Jez, working with the scholars, he believes that if they can grasp how fortunate they are to be doing what they do, it will give them that extra edge in training, that extra 10 per cent when it is necessary. He also believes it keeps them grounded as young men, whether they make it or not as professional footballers.

News broke that week of the death of Rushden & Diamonds goalkeeper Dale Roberts, who had taken his own life following difficulties off the field. It was a tragic end to a young life and a promising career. Having had contact with Roger Knight, the chaplain, quite recently following the conversation with Lance Key at the funeral, I again got in touch pretty quickly and assured him of my prayers. Lance and I had spoken about Dale and some of the challenges that he was facing, and I had sent an email across to Roger just to let him know of this conversation.

The chaplains' network comes into its own at times like this, as players in a number of other clubs were affected by what had happened to Dale. The footballing world is quite a small one, and with players moving around as often as they do, it does mean that events like the one which unfolded at Rushden that week can have a big effect around the country.

On a few occasion over recent seasons I have written a letter to another football club offering our condolences to them on the loss of someone associated with the club. The first letter I was asked to write was to Macclesfield following the death of their manager Keith Alexander. This was followed by a letter to Exeter City on the death of Adam Stansfield, and after Dale's passing I wrote to Rushden & Diamonds. For me this is an important part of the role that I am privileged to fulfil, and in some cases it may open the door for chaplaincy in clubs where there are no chaplains. The ripples of tragic events like these spread very wide, and we can never know just how big an impact small actions and kind words at appropriate times can have.

The Memorial Garden was taking shape, and I had been in contact with local stonemasons Ivett and Reed as they had agreed to produce our memorial stone. I had been a couple of times to proof it and was now informed that it was ready for collection. We had planned to have the opening of the garden on the same day as the Carols at the Abbey event, to tie the two together, but with the weather being as cold and frosty as it was, it was proving to be very difficult to lay the slabs and get the area set correctly. The memorial stone was collected and delivered to the club; all that was needed now was for the weather to turn enough for the rest of the area to be finished.

While at the club, I found myself in the strange position of running the club shop for a couple of hours. As I've mentioned already, by nature, I find it difficult to say 'no' to things, and at the same time, I also want to be a blessing to people. So with my role at United from day one I had always sought to offer practical as well as pastoral help. Over the past five seasons this has led on a number of occasions to me rustling up a team of local young people to help around the ground, including wiping down and cleaning pigeon muck off the seats and washing the advertising boards. On one occasion for a pre-season friendly I ended up selling tickets for the club's income-generating 50:50 draw (half the proceeds form a cash prize for the holder of the winning ticket, the other half going to the club) to the Norwich City fans as the club were really short-staffed. In fact, in lots of little ways just being available and willing to help has had big rewards. And I was now serving in the shop!

In the run up to Christmas, the shop was doing a reasonable amount of business, but sickness and the staff needing to be else-where for a meeting meant that as I walked in, they had no one to cover the shop and faced having to close it for a couple of hours. So instead I spent a couple of hours keeping things ticking over, and even in that short time, was surprised how much business I had. I'm sure it won't be the last time I end up doing something you wouldn't necessarily associate with the chaplain's role – but that's the way I am.

Our next home game against Darlington the week before Christmas was another that fell foul of the weather. Often the pitch will be inspected on the day of the game, but with the prospect of Darlington having to travel down from the north on the Friday and stay overnight the decision was reached earlier to avoid the journey.

A more pressing concern for me was the threat again hanging over the carol service scheduled for the Monday evening. Because it takes place outside, with those attending sitting in the stands, it isn't just about the state of the roads – we have to consider the safety of the paths, the steps up to the stand, the seats and the outside temperature bearing in mind people are going to be sitting there for a while.

All in all, when weighing things up, it was felt to be the right decision to cancel for the second year running. That weekend was a nightmare – we were wrestling with the decision, trying to give the event every opportunity to happen, while at the same time needing to make the decision early enough so that the news could be sent out via the website and the media.

Having had the event cancelled for two years running due to the weather, the validity of the event in its current form was in question – I needed to weigh up the options for a future year. The reality is that the club had no function room large enough to take the number of people we usually attracted. Other clubs that hold carol services have different approaches – they might be hosted in the local church, or one of the club's large function rooms, or they might just have a smaller service for staff, players and families. So what came next for Cambridge United's Carols at the Abbey? This remained an unanswered question, but the truth is that we couldn't keep on as we had in the past two years.

Having discussed the Conference fixture scheduling earlier, there is one very positive thing about it: each year the games on Boxing Day and New Year's Day are played home and away against the local teams. At the start of each season, each club is asked to nominate the club it wants to play on these days – this means less travelling for fans and for players. In the case of Cambridge United this has meant a journey of no more than 45 minutes for the years they have been in the Conference.

With Histon currently in the same division and lying just outside Cambridge the other side of the A14, these Boxing Day and New Year's Day games have taken on extra zest. However, the away game at Histon on Boxing Day was yet another to fall to the weather – the snow and ice had decimated the footballing fixtures through December.

Another problem that faces teams like Cambridge United who do not have their own purpose-built training facilities is that with snow and ice on the ground there is nowhere to train. For the management and coaching staff it becomes a real challenge as, particularly in Cambridge, indoor facilities that can be used for such purposes are few and far between; they are usually attached to schools and therefore accessing them during term time is a real problem.

So the players were at the gym on more than one occasion to keep their fitness levels up. There wasn't opportunity for ball work, but at least the lads were able to do some cardio work. And watching one of these sessions I was again struck by the atmosphere within the group, the banter between management and players and between the senior players and the younger lads. It was a particularly pleasant surprise to see former United player Wayne Hatswell training with the lads. Afterwards I was able to catch up with him. It was almost a year since he had left United and gone to Southern Ireland as player/coach with Dundalk. He had finished his season there and was now back in the UK where he had been appointed player/coach at Newport County, although he hadn't started formally because of the timing of the transfer window. He had been in touch with United about joining them to keep fit, something the management were willing to accommodate, as he and his wife still live in the area.

As has been mentioned many times, football is a small world, and what was happening with Wayne is not unusual – there have been times when players have joined in training just to get fit and to give them an opportunity to find a club. Over the years there have been a number of players that have been with the squad for training while never signing for the club. At a similar time, the national media brought this to attention, reporting on David Beckham training with Tottenham Hotspur.

The weather finally improved, and after an incredible amount of work by Ian, Mick and the team, the game between Christmas and New Year, a home game against Mansfield, was able to go ahead.

Before kick-off, a minute's silence was observed to mark the death of Dale Roberts. The Football Conference had sent an instruction that at the next home game after his death a minute's silence was to be observed, and as the Darlington game had been called off, this game was next. So with the players stood round the centre circle, the stadium stood in silence to remember Dale.

Whenever a minute's silence or applause is observed the League has to be notified. Occasionally instructions will come down from on high – for example, after Alan Ball died in 2007, all football clubs were asked to observe a minute's applause. In the case of Dale the instruction had came from the Conference. If United wish to observe a minute's applause or silence – as in the situation with Harry Williams – the League must be informed, and assuming all is well with them, the opposition and match referee are also asked.

By the end of the 90 minutes, however, it was a game that United fans were wishing had been called off, with Mansfield running out 5–1 winners. Two stunning Mansfield goals put them two up at half time. An equally stunning goal from Robbie Willmott briefly got the U's back into the game. But as they continued to chase the game, gaps appeared at the back and Mansfield netted a third, adding two more in injury time.

The fickle nature of football showed itself again, with fans calling for the manager's head, despite this being the first loss since the beginning of October. It wasn't a great performance, and perhaps showed up the lack of ball work in the preceding weeks. But were Mansfield worthy of a 5–1 win? Probably not on the balance of play – but that is football. Sometimes when you chase the game it pays off, as it did against Tamworth, and yet other times the opposite is true and you end up with a heavier score line. But those are the decisions that a manager is paid to make, and they stand or fall by the outcome of those decisions. Martin Ling was fairly philosophical afterwards.

As a chaplain with ready access to the changing room before and after the game, it is very easy to go in when the players have just won 4–0 and everyone is buoyant. It is something else to be there when they've been trounced 5–1. But I believe it is important that I'm there when it is easy but also when it is hard and no one wants to look you in the eye. At those times, a shake of the hand or a pat on the back is often enough.

The same is true with the management. It would be very easy to come up with reasons not to go into the manager's office when things are going badly, but for me that stinks of hypocrisy. I'm there for when things are good and when things are bad; my role, while it is easier when things are going well, also requires me to be honest when things are tough and not shy away.

As mentioned at the start of the season, having the scholars over to the house has been something Hayley and I have done regularly. With the first team though, it has been a bit hit and miss, but we managed to get a hit this season! So after training the players were duly sent round for a cuppa and piece of cake. On the previous occasions we had done this, the invitation had been given, and some of the players had responded. On this occasion, the lads were 'encouraged' to attend, so barring the few injured players, we had a full house.

As a good number of the lads had come through the youth ranks, they were not on unfamiliar territory – and again, Corban, our youngest, had them on the Wii and took great delight in beating one or two of them at Mario Kart, although I'm sure they'd try to convince you that they let him win. It also gave me the opportunity to talk with one or two of the lads who were perhaps a little more relaxed and in a different environment from the training ground. I also feel it's important for the players to meet my family – not something that naturally happens around training or football matches. This can give us a connection, something in common that we can talk about, and I have found that it does open up some doors that may have otherwise remained closed.

My programme notes for the New Year's Day home match with Histon addressed the difficult question of how we can marry the celebration of Christmas and the birth of Jesus with the reality of life, in the light of the deaths of Dale Roberts and Harry Williams, two young lives tragically cut short. Is it possible to reconcile them?

As a minister there are many times when I need to learn to say nothing. In the line of work I'm in, we've been taught how to speak, what to say and how to say it. But in my limited experience, I am beginning to learn that there are times when saying nothing is actually the best thing to do. It is all too easy to try to explain things and offer words of comfort, when actually words are not the answer. When people are facing difficult times, often they just need to know that someone cares and is there for them. There is a time and place for conversation, but there is also a time and place for simply being there.

And the truth is that God is the model example of how this should be, because the whole point of the Christmas story is summed up in the words found in Matthew's account where he quotes from the Old Testament book of Isaiah: 'All this took place to fulfil what the Lord had said through the prophet: "The virgin will conceive and give birth to a son, and they will call him Immanuel" (which means "God with us").'

Christmas is about God coming to be with us. And as I reflected on the pain and heartache associated with the two tragedies, I was reminded of this truth – God is with us. In the midst of pain, God isn't far away, he is right there in it. Sometimes we find him there and sometimes we're not looking, so we don't. But he's there. As chaplain, it is my prayer that I will not just be the mouthpiece that speaks of God but the hands and feet that demonstrate the truth – God is with us.

The month ended with United through to the second round of the FA Trophy and in the league lying in 13th place with a record of played 22, won 6, drawn 8, lost 8. The unbeaten run had come to an end, and with the weather having lifted slightly, January promised to be a heavy month, with six league games and the FA Trophy trip to Alfreton Town to come.

December Results

Sun 5	Blue Square Bet Premier	**Newport County P United P**
Sat 11	FA Trophy 1st round	**United 2 Forest Green Rovers 1** *Partridge, o.g.*
Sat 18	Blue Square Bet Premier	**United P Darlington P**
Sun 26	Blue Square Bet Premier	**Histon P United P**
Tues 28	Blue Square Bet Premier	**United 1 Mansfield Town 5** *Willmott*

January 2011

The minute's applause in memory of Harry Williams had been arranged for the New Year's Day clash at the Abbey between Histon and United. Harry, as well as being a United fan and playing for St Ives Under-18s had been friends with some of the Histon fans, and so it seemed to be the most appropriate match to hold the minute's applause. I was joined pitchside by a number of Harry's family, and as is usually the case, the moment passed by impeccably. Some of the fans in the Newmarket Road end where Harry used to stand chanted his name, and it was a very moving tribute to a young life tragically cut short.

For most home games, the scholars are in action themselves, playing under the name CRC in the Ridgeons Premier Division. On this occasion, they had no game so they were at the match, as was Jez George. It provided me an opportunity before kick-off to have a chat to Jez about how things were going with the lads, and to arrange an evening for them to come over to the house. At those games where the scholars are present, I do take the opportunity of going and saying 'hi' to them and asking them how they are doing, but usually it is far better to get one or two of them on their own – it is much harder to engage in anything other than a brief 'hello' when they are all sitting together.

The lads did come over for an evening early in the New Year. We had a really good evening with them, the majority of them taking their turn playing on the Wii or playing magnetic darts, but within all of the fun and banter, there were opportunities to talk to one or two about family, about Christmas and about how they were finding things just over halfway through the season. The reality for many of the second years is that come Christmas, they are already starting to think about what happens next. Although the season doesn't finish until the end of April or early May, their college course will be completed and some will have been released from the club by Easter.

So while still enjoying the experience, at this time of year most of the second years are beginning to look ahead to what comes next.

Some are already pretty clued up that they won't be offered a professional contract, while for others there is still something to work for and a decision yet to be made, with the ball firmly in their court to put in a good stint and force their way into the reckoning. There have been a few players that have only really pushed on in those last months and shown that they may have the potential to go further.

Seeing them in a social environment gives me a little more insight into their characters and attitudes and helps me to understand much more readily many of the decisions that are taken with regards to these lads over the offering of development or professional contracts.

The New Year's Day match with Histon ended in a 0–0 draw, the U's finding it very difficult to break down a resolute and determined Histon defence. As was proved earlier in the season with the same score line against Southport, United have often struggled to break down teams that come and play deep with numbers behind the ball. Even the second half dismissal of Histon's Erkan Okay didn't help the United cause.

The fans had been hoping that United would bounce back in style following their below par display against Mansfield, but as this was not forthcoming, large sections of vocal supporters were laying the blame firmly at the door of Martin Ling. To say it wasn't a happy dressing room would be understating it, and Martin was obviously frustrated. However, being a seasoned manager he was well aware of the encouragement needed for the players. On the positive side, they didn't have long to wait to put things right – there was an away trip to Eastbourne Borough on the Bank Holiday Monday. And put it right they did with a 2–0 win, goals coming courtesy of Robbie Willmott and Wayne Gray.

It hadn't been a great Christmas and New Year campaign, with one match postponed, one lost, one drawn and one won. Equally, it wasn't perhaps the great disaster it could have been. The great frustration though, was that the two worst performances had come at home.

A club like Cambridge United, whether they win or lose, will always get a regular number of die-hard fans who will stick by the club whatever, although of course they will be very vocal when things aren't going right. Season ticket sales are usually between 1,000 and 1,200. And there is another group of fans who will be at more games than not. These again are pretty committed to the cause and will also be fairly vocal.

But the club also has a large group of floating fans – these are fans that may turn up once or twice during the season, and are the large pool of fans that enabled the club to take 20,000 fans to Wembley two years running for the play-off finals. If these fans come to a game and see United play well, and things look like they are heading in the right direction, they will usually come back a little more often. It was this group that had swelled the ranks at the recent Boxing Day and New Year's Day matches to between 4,000 and 5,000. However, in the current run of form, United appeared to be playing better away from home, and that wasn't a great recipe for getting fans through the turnstiles.

Over the Christmas 2010/11 campaign United's best gate was 3,225 for the Histon match, a game that a few season back had attracted about 7,000 fans. This was perhaps due to the fact that these two clubs had played each other a few times now so the novelty factor had worn off, and added to that, both clubs' regular attendances had dropped off. Not only were numbers significantly down on previous seasons, but for those who did turn up, what they saw was not the most exciting and encouraging of performances by the U's.

This created added pressure on the manager, because ultimately the club needed the paying fans to come along. It also made it that much more difficult to sell match day hospitality and to develop the corporate and commercial side of the club. As I've mentioned already, I find myself in the privileged position where people will talk to me – whether they are players, management, directors, staff or fans. While I never break confidences, it is unique to hear the range of feelings and pressures felt by all involved with the club. In that place, the best I can offer is to listen and maybe encourage them to think of the perspective of others.

After the Christmas campaign, it wasn't a great surprise when in the first week of January the chairman, Paul Barry, put the club up for sale in a public statement. In reality, nothing much had changed, as Paul had already stated on a number of occasions that if the right person came along and it was in the best interests of the football club he would be willing to consider selling some of his shares in the club.

Paul originated from Cambridge and is a United fan. He had moved to the States but had continued to serve as a director and helped keep the club afloat on many occasions. He had stepped in as chairman, originally in an acting capacity when George Rolls left the club. And he had sought to fulfil this role from his home in Seattle. Putting the club up for sale was an invitation for other possible investors to get involved.

The 'For Sale' sign being put up at United was a big news story in Cambridge that week, and as a result I was contacted to ask whether I'd go in to do a radio interview on the Sunday morning BBC show. Alongside the Jeremy Sallis Show, the Sunday morning programme is one that I usually get asked once or twice a year to do an interview on – and in most cases because of my role at United. I am happy to oblige, although I have noticed that I always seem to get the early slots for some reason!

Back on the pitch, the players followed up their away win at Eastbourne with three points at the other end of the country – Barrow. More goals from Robbie Willmott and Wayne Gray made the long return journey that little bit more bearable.

Because of the way the fixtures work, I only get to relatively few of the games the scholars play, either as CRC or as Cambridge United Youth. So when a chance does arise, it is great for me to be able to be there. One such opportunity arose when the scholars took on Cambridge City in the Cambridgeshire Invitation Cup quarterfinal and so I headed down to watch the game.

I mentioned earlier in the season when travelling to Bury Town that grounds that don't have segregation are great for walking round and chatting to folk. Being a smaller ground, Milton Road, the current home of Cambridge City FC, alongside watching the game, gave me plenty of opportunity to wander about and chat to people, including some of the Cambridge City players not involved, notably Robbie Nightingale who is also the groundsman at Clare College sports ground, the training facilities used by United.

Some of the die-hard United fans were also present, and being in a slightly more relaxed environment provided opportunities to engage in conversation which aren't always possible at United's home games because of match-day duties and other pressures.

Some of the young first team players who had come through as scholars – Darryl Coakley, Blaine Hudson, Adam Marriott, Jordan Patrick and Sam Ives – were also there, and sitting with them during extra time gave me a chance to catch up with their news. These lads, although now on professional or development contracts, had not forgotten their time with Jez, and were supportive of the work he was doing and the new lads coming through as well. It was good to see them giving their encouragement and support to the new batch of talent emerging. CRC ran out 4–3 winners in extra time, progressing to the semi-finals.

Although, unlike with the first team, I won't tend to go into the dressing room with the youth team, I did speak to them all as they left the field after their warm-down. Hanging back for those 20 minutes as all the other fans leave often proves to be well worth it regarding the contact with the players. It also makes a difference to them knowing that I have been to watch them and does help with building relationships in the future.

My contact with the scholars is one of those areas within all of my chaplaincy work that I find most frustrating. This isn't because of the scholars themselves or because of a lack of opportunities, but simply a lack of time – I often think how different things would be if I could spend a little more time with them. Some clubs have chaplains who are only responsible for the academy structures, and other chaplains who do not have the opportunities that I have with the first team or supporters will give more time to the scholars, some even acting as minibus drivers for the lads. But I have to be realistic, and with a family, I cannot be out every Saturday, or every evening either, although at times I'm sure it feels like that to my family.

The 'little and often' contact I do get with the scholars does reap its rewards down the line, as has been shown this season with Josh Coulson, Rory McAuley and others. While it may remain a source of constant frustration, I can only seek to make the most of the few opportunities for greater contact as the season unfolds. I also hope and pray that the little contact that the scholars who don't end up staying at United have with me will not be forgotten as the months and years roll by – certainly there is one ex-scholar I have had some contact with since he left, both by email and text, and when that happens it is a real encouragement.

Following on from the meeting about the club's centenary and the production of the book *Cambridge 'Til I Die*, I set up a meeting between Nigel Ashman from the Youth and Community Trust, myself and a local primary headteacher to talk about the best way of getting the book out into the community, and particularly into schools.

It is great to have ideas and vision, but it is something else to be able to turn those ideas into reality. Having produced the book, it was a great idea to get it into schools and seek to encourage younger boys in particular to pick it up, supporting the national drive for improved literacy, particularly among boys. The actual application of this though was somewhat different, as the book was by and large aimed at an older age group and not at primary school age – the age, according to statistics, that needed to be targeted. And some of the humour and language was a bit grown-up and not suitable for primary school children.

Knowing how schools work and what is appropriate is therefore important. Just as it's no good offering an electrician a spanner when what he needs is a screwdriver, so offering a resource to schools that doesn't fit the bill and do the job is equally no good. While the club might feel it has achieved something by giving away a good number of books, if they would simply end up in a cupboard or most likely on top of a cupboard collecting dust, that isn't any use.

Being independent of CFU enables me at times to pose the appropriate questions and create the appropriate dialogue. The meeting that day with Nigel and the head came about as the two of us were trying to work out how we could facilitate the distribution of these free books in a way that would actually be beneficial. Our suspicions were confirmed as the head agreed the books were not really suitable for primary school age children, except for the occasional group reading in Year 6 (10–11-year-olds) when the appropriate stories to read could be selected.

From day one, I have always seen my role as chaplain not just to be there for the players, but for staff, directors and supporters as well. My work with the players tends to find me at the training ground, but I also make time to drop by the club offices at a time when I hope the staff will not be hugely pressured. Despite my efforts, there have been many times I've popped in when it clearly isn't the right time, or when everyone has gone out! But I do try to make the effort to carve out time to go with no agenda other than to be around for a catch-up and chat if there is anything going on. There are also obviously times when I go in with specific questions, to attend meetings or to have essential conversations.

Over the years there have been a number of occasions when someone has just needed a shoulder to cry on, someone to offload onto or just a smile and a word of affirmation.

This doesn't happen every time I go in to the offices, and it's certainly true that I don't find someone in floods of tears every time! But the times when things are seemingly just ticking along allow my presence there to be seen as normal and so when things do hit, I am available.

Being available for the staff is an important part of my role. Many of the staff work exceptionally hard and long hours; they very often go the extra mile and give over and above what is required of them. However, it does mean that they can be quite susceptible to the odd comment or critical remark and this can occasionally tip them into getting things out of perspective. The words 'thank you' are not heard that often, but when things go wrong then you can be sure the staff will soon hear about it.

The footballing diary doesn't just affect the lives of the players and managers and their families. It also has a big impact on the staff at the club. Being a listening ear is often all that is required and I have been amazed at how much of an impact it can have just to let someone unload. And of course this isn't just true of football – it is true in every walk of life. Our lives are so busy and we increasingly have fewer and fewer people we can be vulnerable and honest with, so we end up carrying more and more stress which in turn has a knock-on effect for our own health and well-being, that of our families and also our places of work. According to the Health and Safety Executive, in 2009/10, an estimated 9.8 million working days were lost through work-related stress. On average, every person experiencing work-related stress was off work for an esti-mated 22.6 days, which equates to 0.42 days per worker.

As chaplain, a significant part of my work is to be there for people should they feel able to and wish to talk. The statistics quoted above demonstrate why there is a growing trend across society for chaplaincy – from the police service to the courts, from council offices to schools. Having someone to offload onto – someone who isn't connected to the organisational structure, man-agement or workforce and is there simply to listen – can be such a relief. And the professional world of sport is no different in its needs from any other sector of society.

One of the passages in the Bible that has had a big impact on my work as a chaplain is the story of Jesus turning water into wine found in John 2. I alluded to this back in July. When we read the story it is all too easy to imagine that Jesus went along to perform a miracle, but in reality he went along to party! He was invited to the wedding celebration and that is why he was there. Time and time again through the accounts of Jesus' life we see him spending time with people – he was definitely a people person. People that society would not listen to, people who had no one that would take the time to hear them unload – these were the people Jesus spent time with. He was the ultimate chaplain!

Only two chapters later in John's account we read about Jesus meeting a woman at a well, and we see here the way he listened and made himself available to listen to her. But the challenge for me when I hear this account is how Jesus then showed how he could help and be the answer to some of her questions and searching. I think I'm OK at doing the listening bit, and allowing people to talk.

But if I'm honest I'm less good at helping people find answers, particularly in Jesus – although I passionately believe he has them!

Back on the pitch, United travelled to Alfreton Town, of the Blue Square Bet Conference North, for the FA Trophy second round match. Alfreton's home form was pretty imperious and they were eyeing up potential promotion to the Blue Square Bet Conference Premier. Goals from Brian Saah, Simon Russell and substitute Adam Marriott meant the game ended in a 3–3 draw and a replay at the Abbey three days later.

This was a blow for me as I had a pre-arranged meeting on that evening. As it happened, I ended up going to the ground, announcing the teams and introducing them onto the pitch before heading off for my meeting – Kieran, our eldest (who, along with Curtis, is a ball boy) kept me in touch with developments via texts. The replay ended the same way as the first game, 3–3, with a goal from Brian Saah and two from Danny Wright taking the game into extra time. However, that is where the run ended with Alfreton adding three more goals in extra time, leaving the final score 6–3, and meaning the U's defence had been breached nine times in the two encounters.

It was a big disappointment as the FA Trophy was felt to be a competition the team could progress in, but it wasn't to be and so United bowed out again in the second round. And yet again a performance at home had been a huge let down – the last three home games had seen United ship eleven goals and score four. So it was no surprise that the fans' frustration increased and the calls for the manager to go became louder.

Words are very easy to say but they can never be taken back. The story is told of an older man who wanted to teach a young man the power of words. He asked him to go and put a feather on the doorstep of each house in the village. When he had done this, the young man came back to the old man and asked him what he should do next. The old man told him to go and collect up the feathers. The young man complained that the wind had blown them all away. The old man turned to him and explained that just like those feathers, once you have spoken words you cannot take them back.

I was reminded again of the power words spoken without thinking can have at the next home game when talking to one of the match-day staff. Comments made in the press had been heard and variously interpreted by members of the match-day staff, and this had caused not a little unease. Communication in any organisation is so crucial, and when it doesn't happen, then you can open the way for misunderstanding and misrepresentation, and end up with a breakdown in relationships. Over the years, this has been the most common complaint that I have ended up talking through with staff – it is not knowing, being kept in the dark and the jumping to conclusions that happens in the absence of anything concrete to go on.

Learning when to keep your counsel and not say anything is as important as knowing when to speak and how to speak. I have worked alongside those who have struggled to keep a rein on their mouths, while others have been too tight-lipped. In a community like Cambridge United Football Club that includes a few thousand people, one or two words spoken out of turn that end up being reported can have a huge effect for good or ill, and in my limited experience it is usually the latter. Listening on that Saturday after-noon, it reminded me again of the need to think through the implications of the words I say and the impact and effect it will have on individuals in particular.

Wrexham were the next team to visit the Abbey. They were a team in a bit of trouble off the field, but on the field they were starting to hit their stride, lying in fifth place in the league and unbeaten in the league for ten games.

Andy Morrell, the Wrexham striker, and Rory McAuley had a clash of heads – Rory was able to be patched up and get back on, but Andy Morrell required stitches and this was done in the medical centre at the ground by the club doctor, Mandy Wharton. As is my usual practice, I followed the player to the medical room to make myself available. I was able to walk Andy back to the away dressing room after he'd been stitched and bandaged up.

On the pitch, things didn't go well again, the U's suffering a 3–1 reverse. Robbie Willmott's stunning free kick in the second half, after United trailed 3–0 at half time, was the only bright spot, and a straight red card for Brian Saah compounded the situation and also rendered him unavailable for the next three games.

The defeat meant that United slipped four places to 14th in the league. There was yet more negative reaction from the fans and the pressure was mounting. Martin Ling remained positive, although naturally frustrated at the mistakes on the pitch that were costing him dear and the seeming lack of good fortune that was besetting him.

From the outset I have purposefully avoided attending AGMs and fans' forums, partly because of time pressures and having to choose where my time should be spent, but also because I have tried to protect my neutral position and by not attending I am able to keep that position clear. The first public meeting that I had attended in my six years took place towards the end of the month – it was a meeting concerning the development and possible relocation of the ground. The meeting had been called by the developers who owned the Abbey Stadium site and I was interested on a couple of accounts to hear what was planned.

Firstly, the ground is near the church I serve and I was therefore interested to hear what impact any development would have on this. If the proposed site for the football club was on the other side of Cambridge, it would change the relationship between the church and the club. While my role would hopefully be safe, the move might have a wider impact. And from a church perspective, any new developments within the local area might have an impact, bringing more homes and community facilities, for example. Secondly, as chaplain, I was interested to hear what consideration, if any, had been given to such matters as the Memorial Garden, and the ashes scattered on the pitch.

It was a very helpful meeting. It was good to be there and to show more than a passing interest in what was going on. There would be work required on my part to ensure that the work done with the Memorial Garden, for example, didn't get lost but was incorporated into any future stadium. I met one of the developers afterwards and asked if I could meet with him at some point, and he was keen to do this.

Travelling to away matches is something that I quite enjoy, as I've mentioned already, because it enables me to watch a game without having duties to attend to. The penultimate game of the month was a Tuesday evening away game against leaders Crawley Town, who were not only beginning to assert themselves in the league but had also knocked Championship side Derby out of the FA Cup to set up a fourth round tie against Torquay United.

Crawley are not an easy side to play against at the best of times, but when they were on such a good run, it was even harder. As has been the case on a few occasions that I have travelled with Martin Ling and the lads I was invited to sit in the dugout – an invitation which I duly accepted.

Wayne Gray had been with the club since the start of the season on a month-to-month contract. He had made 20 appearances and nine as a substitute, and had scored eight goals. However his contract had not been extended due to financial constraints and so he was absent from the party that travelled to Crawley, along with the suspended Brian Saah. I dropped Wayne a text wishing him all the best to which he replied. I don't often get to see players once they've been released and therefore the only way to get hold of them is with a text. Some players will reply and some won't. Often I won't get a player's number until he leaves the club, and then I will ensure I get the number and drop him a text. Alex Stavrinou was another player whose time at United finished during January, as his loan spell from Charlton wasn't extended.

I spent a bit of time chatting with Danny Naisbitt as he sat on the bench – he and Simon Brown had swapped gloves again, Simon Brown being recalled, and it was obvious that there was more to this decision. Danny didn't give anything away and I didn't push, but I was able to talk to him about how he felt in the light of what had transpired.

United defended stoutly in the first half, heading in 0–0 at half time. But Martin Ling's bad luck continued as Dave Partridge, who had been having an immense game at the heart of the defence, limped off in the second half. The enforced substitution unsettled the team and Crawley soon took the lead from a corner kick, punishing the makeshift United defence, before adding two more. The final score showed a comfortable 3–0 win for the home side, which in no way told the full story of the game.

Being in the dressing room before the match, at half time and at the end of the game, I could see it was a bitter pill to swallow for the lads, and not least the management – things were going against them and in the main it wasn't due to bad decisions, but injuries, suspensions and not getting the breaks.

Yet another game had been lost and United went another couple of places down the league table. This season was proving a tough one, and at every turn, Martin Ling's plans were being foiled.

Times like this are really difficult to handle and I find it very hard to process. I'm not into praying for wins – I don't believe that is right. But I was praying that the players played to the best of their ability, with confidence that if that happened and everything else went well, the players were good enough to get results. And yet we had players being sent off, seemingly very harshly; we had players picking up injuries; and in almost every case these were the senior players at the club – the players you needed to have around when your back was against the wall. But what could I do as chaplain? Personally I have never had the experience of having to go through relegation with a team; Cambridge United have always been at this level in the time I have been involved with them as chaplain. But I know that each season some chaplains experience the joy of promotion with their clubs while others face the pain of relegation.

Our presence as chaplains is not to influence results but to be there for people. And yet when you see people hurting and struggling because of circumstances that you are powerless to change it is hard. All I could do was pray for those involved and trust that somehow God would be at work in this situation.

The last match of the month was another away trip (the U's were clocking up the miles on the road this month). This time we were heading west for a trip to Bath City, but without Brian Saah (suspended) or Dave Partridge (injured). Another notable absentee from the squad for the trip was the club's longest serving player, Robbie Willmott. Robbie had completed his transfer to Luton Town after the Crawley Town game. He had been on a rich vein of form, and had been tipped for a move away in the January transfer window, with a number of clubs putting in offers for him.

This is part of the game that I have had to come to terms with. I had known Robbie for five-and-a-half years, from being a precocious talent with the CRC youth team to becoming a regular in the first team. But as he moved on, I hoped that he left with a different view of Christianity as a result of those few years of knowing me in my role. As I always did, I sent a text wishing him well for the future.

And so it was a bare bones team that took to the field against Bath. Young Jonathan Thorpe, starting at right back, was the latest player to fall foul of the officials, with a red card for a fairly innocuous-looking tackle on Kaid Mohamed. A difficult afternoon steadily got worse, Mohamed netting twice as United lost 4–0.

On Monday morning I was back at the training ground to see the players as Martin and John took them for a walk and a talk through the events of the last few days. As Martin said to me, he would just like a break – something to go his way for a change. Why it hadn't I don't know. If I had the answers I'd be a rich and popular man.

But that afternoon, things were put into perspective as I visited the Teenage Cancer Trust centre at Addenbrooke's Hospital to talk through with the staff there what possible links could be developed with the club following the players' visit at Christmas. I went on to meet one of the play team to talk about a six-year-old boy who was now paraplegic following a car accident – again, a little lad that we had met at Christmas. The play team were looking to begin to get him out and about and wanted to know what might be possible with the Cambridge United team. We spoke about him coming along to a home game and meeting the players before kick-off, but decided to wait for the warmer weather before setting this up.

It reminded me again that although football is the livelihood of some people and their wages depends on it, despite Bill Shankly's famous saying, there are more important matters. Yes, the month ended on a pretty poor note for Cambridge United, slipping from 13th to 16th in the table with a record of played 28, won 8, drawn 9 and lost 11. But there were some children and teenagers worse off, whose lives had been destroyed by tragic accident or illness. This was a salutary reminder to keep everything in perspective.

January Results

Sat 1	Blue Square Bet Premier	**United 0 Histon 0**
Mon 3	Blue Square Bet Premier	**Eastbourne Borough 0 United 2** *Willmott, Gray*
Sat 8	Blue Square Bet Premier	**Barrow 1 United 2** *Willmott, Gray*
Sat 15	FA Trophy 2nd round	**Alfreton Town 3 United 3** *Russell, Saah, Marriott*
Tues 18	FA Trophy 2nd round (replay)	**United 3 Alfreton Town 6** (aet) *Saah, Wright 2*
Sat 22	Blue Square Bet Premier	**United 1 Wrexham 3** *Willmott*
Tues 25	Blue Square Bet Premier	**Crawley Town 3 United 0**
Sat 29	Blue Square Bet Premier	**Bath City 4 United 0**

February 2011

Due to fixture rescheduling, the first two games of the month of February were the away and home fixtures against Rushden & Diamonds, both played within five days of each other. The second of these two, the home fixture, had been selected as the match to mark LGBT month as part of the continuing 'Kick It Out' campaign. So the month began with a photo at the Abbey with the 'One Game, One Community' flag and various members of the LGBT organising committee, along with representatives of the club.

Their attendance at the game was generally well received, with only one or two comments made as leaflets were refused. They couldn't believe how few of their leaflets had ended up on the ground – they were anticipating a much harsher response. They had genuinely been surprised at how well they had been received, and were encouraged by the atmosphere they had experienced. For many of those attending it was their first game at the club, and they had been pleasantly surprised. It proved to be a very useful and productive contact and a further step along the road to the club fully embracing the 'Kick It Out' campaign. There was still work to do, but I did feel as though progress was being made and recognition for our work with the campaign was an achievable ambition.

Following the photo I took the opportunity to catch up with Greg and James Wynne, the kit manager, as they prepared to leave for Rushden. But I was not expecting what followed – as I stood talking to Greg and James, Martin Ling walked out of the boardroom, having just been relieved of his duties. He shook our hands, thanked us all for our support and left with a promise to come back for a drink sometime. He was naturally upset, but that was it. The contracts of Martin and John Schofield had been terminated.

We stood there not quite sure what to say and how to respond to one another. Having watched the recent games feelings of frustration emerged again – the sending offs, the injuries, things seemingly working against Martin at every turn. My heart went out to him – he had given the club his best and worked to develop a set of lads who should have been pushing for a play-off place, and yet here we were with three months of the season to go, with him having lost his job and the club lying in 16th place.

The season had started so optimistically, the new players who had arrived, along with first team coach John Schofield, had settled quickly and there was some very nice football being played. But one thing after another had robbed Martin of the success he was building towards. It is often said that a team's luck balances itself out over the course of the season, but at this point of the season, I couldn't see how that would be the case. Certainly Martin's luck seemed to have run out completely – the heady night of that 'Oh so nearly' game at Huddersfield had evaporated in a matter of weeks.

And so the merry-go-round of new managerial appointments began. After my initial shock, and concerns about the impact on players and the club as a whole, my thoughts turned to myself and my role. I had been so thankful for my good relationship with Martin – what would my relationship with the new manager be like? I had heard stories of chaplains having doors closed to them following new managers arriving and changing the way things worked – was that going to be my experience?

A change in manager is unsettling for everyone, although those least affected are perhaps the fans. For staff, there needs to be a new relationship established – trust needs to be built up, and often a manager's relationship with other staff will depend very heavily on their experiences to date. A positive relationship with staff in a former club will most likely lead to a positive relationship in the new club, whereas if the manager felt he was undermined at his previous club, he will naturally be very wary and suspicious coming into the new one.

For players, one manager's style isn't necessarily the style of another and therefore one manager's first choice will not necessarily be another's. And the same feelings are there for the chaplain too – after all we are human beings and are just as affected by change as everyone else.

In the short term it was announced that Jez George and Nolan Keeley would step in to run the first team affairs with Marc Tracy, Tom Pell, James Cutting and the rest of the youth development team taking on additional responsibilities to release Jez and Nolan.

The away game at Rushden is usually one that I try to get to as it is close and I know the chaplain well. However, although I had planned to go to the original game, the rearranged match clashed with another meeting and so I was unable to make it.

On the pitch things started out well for the U's with them taking an early lead through Danny Wright. But then the bad luck that had haunted Martin Ling struck again, with first James Jennings and then Simon Russell substituted because of injury. United ended the game with a very youthful-looking side, with seven of the eleven being products of the youth scheme under Jez. Unfortunately, Rushden got a late winner to take a 2–1 victory on the night.

The return leg a few days later was equally frustrating for the U's, Rushden running out 2–0 winners. As a result of this, their fifth successive league defeat, the U's slipped a place to 17th.

The Rushden & Diamonds chaplain, Roger Knight, attended the game at the Abbey, and so I invited Roger to walk round with me and to come on the pitch. Roger introduced me to the Rushden physio, who was out on the pitch for the warm-up. It was also good to catch up with Lance Key, the Rushden goalkeeping coach – this was the first time I'd seen him since Dale's death before Christmas.

As a positive demonstration of our relationship as chaplains, when it came to reading out the teams I introduced Roger as the Rushden chaplain and let him read out the Rushden team, while I read out the Cambridge team. Interestingly, Roger got a spontaneous round of applause from the Rushden fans after he'd finished reading the team out – a point I made to the home fans when I had finished the United team!

There were also a couple of ex-United players in the Rushden team – Max Porter had been with us for a few months early on in my time at the club. He had eventually landed at Rushden where he had become a firm favourite. While there he had also been called up to play for the England C international side. The England C team features players who play for clubs outside the Football League. They play full internationals as the top pros do, get caps and are treated in exactly the same way. It is an honour that a few of the United lads have received over the years. As a result of Max being in the England team he was very close to Dale Roberts (also an

England C international) and his death had had a big impact on Max. It was great to have a good catch-up after the game.

Another ex-United lad in the Rushden team was Michael Gash. Michael had signed for Cambridge United from Cambridge City and then, following a spell back at Cambridge City, had gone on to play for Ebbsfleet United before signing for York. He was on loan at Rushden from York.

Losing twice to Rushden in a week was a blow, but there were signs that some of the younger lads coming in could do a good job. The hard work for Jez and Nolan would begin now as they sought to make their mark on the squad and get things set up as they wanted them. At just the right time for them there was no midweek game, giving them a full week of training to get the lads set up for the next match.

I was able to pop in for part of that first morning after the second Rushden match and to see Jez and Nolan begin to put their stamp on things. It was interesting, being around the players and gauging the different responses to Jez taking it on – some were sceptical and uncertain as to what it might mean for them, while others were more positive as they saw an opportunity for themselves to push for a place. One of the notable absentees from the training that morning was assistant manager Paul Carden, and it soon emerged that he had gone on loan to Luton Town until the end of the season.

There is a saying, 'A week is a long time in football' and it is so true – one week you can be a hero, the next a villain. One week you can be out of favour, the next in the starting eleven. With the new temporary management team in place, players faced up to the opportunities that this brought them. Josh Coulson was installed by Jez George as his new captain – it was a great week for Josh as he'd also received a call up to the England C team.

Reflecting on the way different people responded to the management change, it struck me again how fragile life can be when we find our security and sense of purpose from circumstances and even from human relationships. For some players, being in the team and playing is what provides them with that security and confidence. But strip that away and their confidence goes, as does their security. How many other people in our world today is this true for? Their security and confidence is based upon a career, a position of responsibility, relationships, and perhaps for some even the size of their bank balance, their house and the possessions they own.

One of the most amazing things about God is he doesn't value us based on what we have achieved or what we have stored up; he doesn't value us because we're playing or because we're not; he doesn't value us because our lives are 'successful' or because they're not. God's view of us is unchanging and is not based on results or a set of pre-defined criteria. It is based purely and simply on the fact that we are made in his image!

And as those made in his image, we were made for a relationship with him and it is in God that we find our true value, security and purpose. As a Christian, this truth is liberating – I am free from having to prove myself, from having to achieve, from having to do this or that – because God loves me and values me for who I am.

Having said that, my human nature does still look for security in these other things, and the trouble for me begins when I give more weight to them than I do to how God views me. So facing up to the prospect of a new manager, I was reminded again that my value is not based upon how they would view me – it is secure in how God sees me.

The relationship I share with Roger Knight at Rushden & Diamonds is one of a number I have with other chaplains. As I have described previously, SCORE chaplaincy, as an organisation, arranges chaplains' get-togethers three times a year. The first is the conference at Lilleshall for all chaplains. The other two meetings are regional ones, and as Cambridge United is classed as being in the same region as Rushden & Diamonds, I meet up with Roger here too. Our spring gathering was at Franklin Gardens, the home of Northampton Saints Rugby Football Club, and a few of us met up over coffee and lunch to share news and stories, to talk about chaplaincy development and to hear about how SCORE was finding answers to some of its fundraising challenges.

SCORE has a number of staff, all practitioners, but who are also working to develop chaplaincy across the country and across the sports. The support and contact I have received through SCORE has been a real help. The sharing of good practice I have found very useful, and I have learnt much from how other chaplains serve in their clubs.

It was following a coffee I had with Matt Baker, who is the pastoral support director for English football and also serves as the chaplain to Charlton Athletic, that I added something new to my role on match days. Matt was chatting to me about his match-day experience and what he does on match days, and as part of his regular pattern he pops in to introduce himself to the referee and his assistants. He also mentioned that he tries to make himself known to the opposition management.

Following that, I began to add visiting the referees to my match-day routine. I had previously done this if there was a minute's silence or applause, just to be clear how the referees wanted that moment to be led. I had already been in the habit of introducing myself to some of the visiting staff during the warm-up.

Another of the great features of the SCORE network is the opportunity to follow up former players as they move on from club to club. For example, when I met up with Tim O'Brien, one of the co-chaplains to Wycombe Wanderers, at a conference, I was able to have a long chat with him about an ex-United player, Scott Rendell, who was now their top scorer for the 2010/11 season. I had enjoyed a good relationship with Scott and had kept in touch with him once he went off to Peterborough. He had come back briefly on loan to United and had then gone out on loan to Torquay. Scott had been through a difficult personal time which I had heard about through people at United still in contact with him, and it was good to be able to hear from Tim how Scott was doing and also to pass on my best wishes to him.

There are one or two other players that I keep in touch with who have moved on from the club, and I find it helpful to try to keep track of some of their movements in order to follow them up, especially where there has been more significant contact and conversation. I believe it is important to foster good relationships with other chaplains, both to share good practice and because in these pastoral situations we can support each other and prayer for one another.

With the benefit of SCORE and their resources – primarily the many chaplains serving round the country – I keep an eye open on the clubs where there are presently no chaplains, especially at the level United play at. This sometimes leads to a conversation with an ex-player or with officials of the club. I do believe in the role of the chaplain and the value of chaplaincy and so I am very keen and willing to encourage other clubs to consider the role.

Two elderly Cambridge United fans passed away during the month – the first was a member of the VP (Vice-Presidents) club and the second was the godfather of a former club commercial manager. In these situations I seek to represent the club as best as I can. In the case of the first gentleman I was unable to attend his funeral, but I rang and spoke to his widow and followed this up with a letter sent on behalf of the club. In the case of the second gentleman I did actually attend the funeral, having spoken to his daughter.

It reminded me again of the privilege of being allowed into the grief of families who have lost loved ones. It was also helpful to be informed of both of these deaths before the funeral – often it has been the case that I have heard after the event. By being aware of the situation beforehand I was able to phone and pass on the condolences of the club. I recognise that in a smaller club the opportunities for this to happen are much greater than in the bigger clubs and it is much easier to provide this personal touch. But however brief the contact, I believe it is important that whoever has the responsibility of helping the club handle these significant life (and death) moments (and in most cases, this will be the chaplain) does so in a thoughtful and appropriate way.

These contacts also acted as a spur to get the Book of Remembrance established and the Memorial Garden finished. The Book of Remembrance was finally ordered during the month. Establishing this book at the club would be the culmination of discussions we had had over a number of seasons .

Six months into the season, the Smile Scheme had raised over £5,000, a not insignificant sum, for local charities, and it was felt right to give the sponsors Marshall Ford a bit of a plug and do a press release with a photo profiling all that had happened during the season so far. We took stock of what had been happening and how things had been working – what could we improve on? It was also an opportunity to begin to plan ahead.

Being involved in this work has been great for increasing the profile of chaplaincy through the various links with charities and businesses. Personally it has been good to support Martin Jordan in his role, and to help the club engage more widely with the local community. Some clubs have a nominated charity of the season and they are able to raise a large sum of cash for that charity. With the way United's Smile Scheme had been structured, by the end of the season we would have benefited over 25 charities with different levels of support.

As mentioned last month, I try to pop in to the club offices from time to time, sometimes with something to ask and sort out or occasionally just as I'm driving past. On one such occasion, as I dropped by, I was able to meet our new loan signing, Ricky Wellard, who had come in on loan from AFC Wimbledon. I didn't know he was there, or even that we'd signed anyone, but as it happened we met as he was filling in the papers.

Although the transfer window had closed there was a further opportunity for loans to be arranged and for clubs in the situation like we found ourselves in, it is really important to have that option. Over the years there have been many, many players who have passed through the club on short-term loans. More often than not teams higher up in the league structure want their players to get some match experience and so will let them go to clubs playing at a lower level, where they may be more likely to be guaranteed a starting place. In some cases those players have gone back to their home clubs and gone on to perform really well. At other times they have struggled to fit back in and end up moving on once their contract has expired.

Ricky had signed in time for him to be in the starting eleven for the trip to Grimsby. It was a game where we defended well and grabbed a deserved point courtesy of a thumping strike by Josh Coulson. Despite the point the U's remained in 17th place.

Back at training there was an opportunity to catch up with Daryl Clare. Daryl had had a frustrating season since signing from Mansfield, although he'd been on loan at Gateshead last season. An obvious talent, he had arrived at United raring to go, but very quickly during pre-season broke down with an injury that took a few weeks to get sorted. This had put him back a bit and he had never really got started.

Daryl had always been chatty and friendly even when things weren't going well for him. And with the new caretaker management in place he had been told he could go out on loan. Naturally disappointed at not being able to get a look in at United, he was very matter-of-fact about his situation, having been round long enough to know how the football world is. Daryl managed to sort out a loan deal with Alfreton Town. He remains a contracted Cambridge United player, and who knows what that will mean come pre-season?

Because of the training schedule, I also had an opportunity to catch up with the youth team goalkeeping coach Martin Davies. Martin has been around for a few years now and had been playing for CRC until injury had sidelined him. He continues to come in a day or two a week to coach the scholars' keepers and also work with the senior goalkeepers. Martin has been helping out with the CRC team for a little while, and although not able to play, can offer Marc Tracy assistance on the touchline. It was good to hear from him of how things were progressing with the scholars, who was stepping up and who was struggling.

Next up at United was an evening game, the rearranged home fixture with Darlington. United started brightly and were awarded a penalty when Luke Berry, making his third start under Jez George, was bundled over. However, his spot kick was saved and Darlington went on to grab the winner, running out 1–0 winners. It was a disappointing end to a game which the U's had had the chance to win.

The evening provided me the opportunity to catch up with the injured players – Adam Miller, Simon Russell, James Jennings and Dave Partridge. They are required to report for the games as well, even though not involved, unless Greg instructs them not to. He will normally get them in early and treat them before the rest of the squad turn up, so by the time the other lads arrive and start to get changed, they have finished their treatment and are often showered and back in their tracksuits. It does mean that if I'm not rushing around doing other things, I can get to catch up with how they're doing and how the injury is progressing, and find out a little about their rehab and how things are outside of the club.

The second Christians in Sport event of the season included an interview with ex-pro footballer Cyrille Regis. I had heard Cyrille speak a few years before and knew he was a very good communicator. On this occasion, Greg and Jez were unable to attend but I took three of the younger lads and an ex-pro friend along. It was an excellent night, and after it I arranged to meet up with one of the lads for a chat as he had clearly been affected by what he had heard.

Cyrille Regis had been a party animal, living the high life as a professional footballer until his best mate in the game, Laurie Cunningham, was killed in a car smash whilst driving under the influence. This brought Cyrille to a crisis moment when he began asking the big questions of life – 'Who am I?' and 'What happens when I die?' – and this process had eventually led to him becoming a Christian.

So I sat in a coffee shop with this lad and we chatted about God, the Bible and Church in a way that in six years I had never done before with any of the players. He asked questions about the church at Barnwell and at the end I was able to offer him a copy of the New Testament, which he took along with a little booklet about being a Christian. And I also had a similar conversation with the other friend I'd brought along. All the lads that attended the evening commented on how good an evening it was.

Afterwards I met Graham Daniels for a coffee and asked him how these evenings could be linked more closely with my work at United – would it be possible to host an evening with Cyrille at the club? Graham was really positive about the idea and we spoke at some length about this. A number of other ideas and possibilities emerged from that coffee with Graham, and left me pondering future opportunities.

The next game United faced was a home game against Kidderminster Harriers – this had been moved to the Friday evening and was the first league game to be screened live from the Abbey. Kidderminster were on a roll and were now pushing for a play-off spot. Before kick-off during the warm-up I got to speak to ex-United captain and now Kiddie player Mark Albrighton, and it was good to have such a warm conversation after a couple of seasons of not having seen him.

United played really well and dominated the game, despite the teams' relative league positions. However, they couldn't find the breakthrough and eventually Kidderminster took the lead against the run of play. Adam Marriott came on as a substitute and scored with a peach of a free kick right at the death. However, United committed the cardinal sin of switching off and Kiddie stole the winner within moments of the restart in added time, claiming a 2–1 win.

Although the performances were improving, Jez was still looking for his first win – so far there was only the point from Grimsby to show for all his hard work. But the fans were responding well to the improved grit and determination being shown by the team and, although secretly wondering how long this could go on, they were pleased that the lads who had come in were doing a good job for the side.

Two more players arrived on loan, Shaun Jeffers from Coventry and Dan Walker from Luton Town. There was another injury, this time to Josh Coulson, but fortunately Dave Partridge had returned. These changes were reflected in the team that travelled the couple of miles to Histon for the rearranged away fixture.

I went along to watch the game standing with the Cambridge United fans, something I do from time to time. I believe it gives me another perspective in my role, and it does open up conversations with different people. I enjoy the opportunity to be part of the Cambridge United community in this way. It was a massive game for both clubs – a win for Histon would see them edge closer to

United and drag us further into the relegation zone – a win for Cambridge and we'd put a little distance between ourselves and those at the bottom.

Cambridge played really well – they dominated the game and created a few good chances. It was goalless at half-time, but in the second half goals from Danny Wright and Adam Marriott sealed a 2–0 win – the first win and the first clean sheet for Jez.

I waited at the end till all the fans had left and then was able to get round to see the players and shake their hands as they left the pitch after their warm-down. It was also good to be able to see Nolan and have a chat to him. After the game Jez is usually in demand from the media for interviews, whereas Nolan doesn't have quite the same pressure, so I am usually able to have a little more time with him.

There is also some history between me and Histon. Before getting involved with Cambridge United, I used to attend a few Histon games because I knew the manager and a few of the players used to coach our boys and run the after-school clubs for them. I can remember being at some of Histon's end-of-season games when they claimed the title and promotion, and enjoyed long FA Cup runs. I also knew the chairman, Gareth Baldwin and his wife Lisa, then Histon's club secretary, through links with Graham Daniels. (Gareth and Lisa had subsequently left Histon and become involved with Cambridge United.)

After I approached Cambridge about the chaplaincy there was a six-month spell when it all went quiet and in that time I spoke to Gareth about chaplaincy at Histon. And in the 2005/06 pre-season when Brian Attmore came to talk to me about chaplaincy at United, I also had an offer from Gareth at Histon to become the chaplain there! I had to make a decision between Histon and Cambridge. To be honest, at that time my heart had said Histon – I knew Gareth and Lisa, the manager Steve, quite a few of the players. But my head said Cambridge United as the club was located in the same area as my church ministry. I spoke to Gareth and explained my dilemma but promised I would find a chaplain for Histon, which I subsequently did through the local Baptist minister, Ron Day.

So although there is local rivalry between the two clubs, I do still know a few of the folk involved at the club, although sadly, things have changed quite dramatically for them in recent seasons and many of those I knew at the club have left. There are still some familiar faces, so when I go back I do try to seek them out and wish them well.

The final Saturday of the month saw the game against Luton rearranged due to their involvement in the FA Trophy. So the month ended with statistics of played 34, won 9, drawn 10, lost 15. United remained in 17th place on 37 points as the season moved towards its penultimate month. There were still many more twists and turns to come, for sure. But finally the hard work Jez and Nolan had been putting in appeared to be reaping rewards.

February Results

Tues 1	Blue Square Bet Premier	**Rushden & Diamonds 2 United 1**
		Wright
Sat 5	Blue Square Bet Premier	**United 0 Rushden & Diamonds 2**
Sat 12	Blue Square Bet Premier	**Grimsby Town 1 United 1**
		Coulson
Tues 15	Blue Square Bet Premier	**United 0 Darlington 1**
Fri 18	Blue Square Bet Premier	**United 1 Kidderminster Harriers 2**
		Marriott
Tues 22	Blue Square Bet Premier	**Histon 0 United 2**
		Wright, Marriott

March 2011

Last summer when I had spoken to CFU about possible links with the community, alongside suggesting taking a lead in the 'Kick It Out' campaign, I had also suggested that they could look at how the club could engage with Fairtrade Fortnight.

Cambridge holds Fairtrade status as a city, and as part of that there is a Fairtrade steering group that meets to help encourage the city to increase access to Fairtrade goods.

I was aware of this group's existence and had been in touch with the chair, a retired Baptist minister, on a few occasions. Fairtrade Fortnight takes place annually at the beginning of March and it was my hope that Cambridge United could get involved and lend its name and support to the efforts of others in the city.

Working with Tom Taylor, who serves with both CFU and the Fairtrade steering group, we set some targets – a Fairtrade line on the tea bars at the ground, talking to our caterers about using Fairtrade coffee, a press release, looking at what the club shop stocks, and possibly devising a school assembly on a Fairtrade theme with a couple of the players.

So as we began March, a press release was issued stating Cambridge United's support for Fairtrade fortnight and Cambridge's status as a Fairtrade city. Although not all of our hopes and aspirations were met, it was a good start; the tea bars were willing to put in a Fairtrade line, our caterers confirmed they used Fairtrade coffee, and I took two of the injured players, Josh Coulson and Adam Miller, into Fen Ditton Primary School to do an assembly about Fairtrade.

I have had the privilege on a few occasions to take school assemblies with some of the players. One, with U's player Andy Duncan, addressed football-related bullying in the playground, and another, with Dan Gleeson, was on the subject of setting targets and goals, not just in football but in life as well. Dan spoke about playing for England C and showed off a couple of the England C caps he had won. I also did an assembly at the start of the academic year with Andy Parkinson – he was talking about handling new beginnings and changes, as he had just moved south with his family and was playing for a new team.

In most cases, these requests come to me as people know of my role as the chaplain, either personally or through another contact. Occasionally a request for the players to attend will come to the club and, depending on what it is that they are being asked to do, this will dictate whether I am involved or not.

While I am very happy and willing to help serve the club in this capacity (within reason of course, recognising I have a church to lead), I have found that my awareness of requests coming to the club over the years has depended largely on the relationship that I have with the staff in the offices. As I am not an employed staff member and I am not in the office most days, there are times when opportunities will pass me by. But I have noticed that as staffing levels have changed and as the staff seek to delegate more, I have become a little more on the radar as someone who can pick up some of the slack.

The local schools are very much on Nigel Ashman's mind as an area for the Youth and Community Trust to engage more fully with. It will be great for me to be able to support this and also to work with the Trust in developing new links where I am able.

This season I had been working closely with Claudine Bone, the club's commercial manager, on the Smile Scheme particularly, but also on one or two other ideas for how I could support her in her work. Will Jones, the club's PR, marketing and media manager, had been involved with the Smile Scheme, and with other developments such as the 'Kick It Out' campaign and Fairtrade Fortnight. He had also been the one to inform me about some of the deaths associated with the club.

I had also had the opportunity to liaise with other office staff members – for example, Lisa Baldwin (club secretary), Claire Osbourn (assistant club secretary) Julie Ankers (youth administrator) and Robert Smith (general manager) – on various matters. The club are also very fortunate to have regular volunteers who come in to help, which is a real bonus, and I have a good relationship with many of these too.

But changes were afoot – Lisa and Robert had both tendered their resignations for the end of the season, and were finishing at the end of April with the last game of the season against Fleetwood Town.

How things would be organised after that date was yet to be seen, and there would inevitably be more changes. As I've mentioned previously, changes in staff have proved a challenge in the past, and in many ways, it makes my role that much more fluid as trust, rapport and understanding need to be re-established. It is part of the world of football that at most clubs this appears to happen on a regular basis on the footballing side – players, coaches and managers are always coming and going. But having a similar turnover with the non-playing staff creates an extra challenge. When people who I have built up a good rapport with leave, there is that very human response of disappointment, uncertainty and to some extent nervousness that doors will close and opportunities will be taken away. The opposite can also be true – it remains to be seen which way things will go at the end of the season.

The first game of the month for United was a second away trip west. This was another rearranged fixture, the trip to Newport County. Dean Holdsworth, who was manager of Newport when they visited earlier in the season, had since moved to Aldershot, and former United man Wayne Hatswell had found himself quickly promoted to number two. Since Dean's departure they hadn't been doing so well.

United took a point, a Simon Russell goal helping them to a 1–1 draw, although arguably it could have been all three if the referee had not overruled his assistant who flagged for a penalty for United in the last minute. Sadly Simon picked up an injury, which would keep him out for the rest of the season. But with that point, United moved up a place to 16th.

Following the lads' visit to Addenbrooke's Hospital and my subsequent meeting with the play workers about young Tobias, we began working towards bringing him along to a game at the end of month.

It would involve him being brought to the ground in his wheelchair, along with his dad and a nurse. Because of his disabilities and the nature of a match day, we had to work out how we were going to put the best experience we could in place for him. One of the youth team coaches Alex Kauffman had helped me out on a few occasions with pre-match or half-time activities, and he agreed to look after Tobias and his party during their visit.

Alex and I went to visit Tobias in hospital and he was really excited about the idea of coming to a match. We met his dad too (on the previous occasions I'd visited, his mum had been there). Plans were in place but it would be dependent on how Tobias was doing healthwise – it could be a long afternoon which might prove too tiring for him.

At our home match on New Year's Day, the charity we had chosen under our Smile Scheme was Magpas Helimedix, a charity that provides critical on-the-spot emergency care – in effect taking the A&E department to where the patients are. They use vehicles and helicopters to transport medics around the area. The medics are all volunteers but the medication they carry, the support staff and the transport all cost money. Following the collection, I began conversations with their fundraiser about other ways in which the club could support Magpas, as they were facing a funding shortfall. As a result, we started to get more involved in a couple of ways.

First of all, Martin Jordan, Josh Coulson and I went up to the Magpas base and were shown around – we got to see the team as they rushed out for a job and met them on their return, when there was a photo opportunity with them and Josh presented the cheque from the Smile Scheme collection. It was interesting to get a behind-the-scenes look at the base. Magpas share the police helicopter and their base is in the same building it operates from. At the end of our visit, the club was presented with a limited edition print of the police helicopter, which we hope to display in our hospitality area. Josh also referred to the visit in his weekly captain's column in the local paper, tweeted about his visit and linked up with Magpas on Facebook.

The following week, Magpas were launching their new fundraising initiative, a lottery, and we arranged for them to come to the club and have the photo shoot on the pitch, with the mayor of Cambridge, some of the Magpas team and some of the United players. It was very pleasing to be able to help in these ways – it was so simple, with little time commitment, but went a long way towards demonstrating that the club is serious about supporting our local community.

Each season, there are a few away games when the players travel on the Friday and stay overnight before the game the Saturday afternoon. During the 2010/11 season we had more of these 'overnighters' than in previous seasons with the games at Wrexham, Fleetwood, Gateshead, Barrow, Darlington and Southport all qualifying. On top of that the Newport game would have been an overnighter if it had been played on the Sunday as originally scheduled, but with it being moved to an evening midweek match, the lads travelled down on the day.

I have in the past travelled on three of these trips, visiting Accrington Stanley, Exeter City and Torquay United. I have found they have provided some good opportunities to talk to the lads and particularly the management over meals and while stretching our legs at service stations and at the hotel. I had hoped to be able to travel again this season, but unfortunately my plans were scuppered with a busy schedule around these games. The lads continued to clock up the miles early in the month, following up the away trip to Newport with games at Darlington and Southport.

Darlington away proved to be another disappointing afternoon, with the U's slipping to a 1–0 defeat. This was followed up with an away game at Southport – this was a massive game, with both clubs at the wrong end of the table. Southport took the lead and things got worse for United as they were reduced to ten men with Adam Marriott's sending off, but Luke Berry snatched a late equaliser to rescue a point.

There was another loan arrival at the U's between these two games. Mark Bentley, the former Gillingham captain had struggled to break back into the side following an injury and came to the U's on loan, bringing with him vast experience. His addition to the squad would prove crucial at just the right time. I caught up with Mark on his first day at training, which just happened to be one of the days that I popped over to Clare College, and I was able to introduce myself to him.

From time to time, some of the students in training at Cambridge's two theological collages, Ridley Hall and Westcott House, will get in touch and ask if they can meet up with me to find out a little more about my work as chaplain to the football club. During the month I had two such conversations. The first was with a lady from Newcastle, a season ticket holder at St James' Park who was training at Westcott House. She had been in touch as she needed to do some placement time, and was curious as to how my work came about and what it involved.

I met Kate at the ground while the photo shoot was happening for the Magpas lottery, and then we headed off for a cup of tea and for more questions. She was interested to know about the relationship between the church and the football club, about how my time was allocated and who dictated what time I gave.

Many of her questions were being asked from the perspective of a parish vicar or curate – as a Baptist minister I am not subject to quite the same pressures. For the vast majority of chaplains, their work in the club – in whatever sport – is not something they are employed to do. They will have a paid role elsewhere, most commonly with a church, but in some cases other paid employment.

I am very grateful that Barnwell Baptist Church are so supportive of my work and see my role as chaplain at the club as an extension of my ministry at the church and in the community. Of course there are times of tension, but because of the positive attitude the church has towards the role, these are often easily sorted out. Different churches and different traditions will undoubtedly have different approaches – I am thrilled with the supportive leadership team I work with and church that I serve. Their generous spirit towards the work has been repaid considerably by the fact that the church has seen numerical growth because of the role – a number of folk have begun to attend as a direct result of my work as chaplain and the contacts that this brings. Had there not been those encouragements, would the church still be as gracious? I couldn't say categorically, but I would hope it would be the case.

Kate then attended the next home match to see how the role worked out on a match day, shadowing me as I walked round the ground and met the various staff and volunteers, although she didn't make it to the dressing room!

A few days later I met up with a colleague of Kate's. James was not after placement time, but an interview to help him with one of his MA essays. So we met in a coffee shop, I answered his questions and we spoke again about the role, how it had developed and the ongoing relationship between church and club.

I often say to these students that becoming chaplain at the football club was the best thing I have ever done as far as my work as a Baptist minister is concerned. One of the dangers in working within a church is you can become surrounded by Christians and separated from the real world. Getting involved at Cambridge United was like a breath of fresh air as it put me in touch again with people living lives outside the world of the church, and for me it acted as a wake-up call to ensure that people can relate to what I do.

It can become all too easy to sit in an office surrounded by books and write a sermon that has no relation to the real world. Being involved with United has given me, I believe and hope, an earthiness to my work in church that makes it accessible to everyone. For example, I sometimes think when preparing for a service how I would feel if one of the players walked in – would they be able to relate to what I was saying and what was happening? Having the opportunity to encourage students in training has been something I have really enjoyed and I hope the lessons to be learnt from chaplaincy will help them as they graduate and find their own parishes or churches.

When it was announced that the Luton game had been moved because of their involvement in the FA Trophy, I knew I had a clash and I wondered how on earth I could get out of it. I had been booked for some time to go to Chatteris and speak to a men's group from the local church about my role as chaplain to Cambridge United. It was strange to think that I'd be sitting with these ten gentlemen talking about what I could have been doing at that moment back at the Abbey as United hosted Luton. But having accepted the booking months ago, I felt I needed to honour the commitment, and so I went to Chatteris and had a good evening with the men. They were encouraged by what I shared, and I hoped it will lead to a few of them coming to the occasional game.

I was disappointed to miss the game as Luton boasted ex-U's Robbie Willmott, Dan Gleeson and Danny Crow, along with Freddie Murray (who had left before I started at United). The current U's assistant manager Paul Carden, on loan at Luton, was eligible to play as there was nothing in his contract to state he couldn't. (There's a future sports quiz question for you – which football player played against the team he was still contracted to as assistant manager?). Ex-United boss Gary Brabin was the Luton number two, so there were a few old friends it would have been nice to catch up with.

On the field, the players put in arguably one of their best performances of the season, the final score being a 0–0 draw, but with both sides having the chances to win it. At the start of the month it was a game we would have been surprised to take anything away from, but a great effort by the lads earned a well-deserved point.

The follow-up to this game was another home fixture against play-off-chasing York City. There was a good crowd in for a special day with our stadium and Smile Scheme sponsors, and the lads followed up the draw with Luton with a fine display, earning a 2–1 win, with Liam Hughes scoring his first goal for the club and the winner coming from Danny Wright.

It was another strong performance, the lads worked hard and the game was only soured by another injury, this time to Luke Berry, which it was expected would keep him out for the rest of the season.

It had been a fantastic week for Liam, a third-year development contract player. While the first team were at Southport, Liam had been playing as centre half for CRC at home to Kirkley & Pakefield in the Ridgeons League Premier Division. But because of Maz's sending off and subsequent suspension, Liam had been brought into the first team for the game against Luton to play up front, and was awarded the man of the match for that game. A few days later, in the game against York City, he got his first goal for the club in only his second start. As is so often said, a week is a long time in football!

Jez and Nolan had worked hard over the years to develop players who, when the need was there, could step up and make the grade. Although it had been a tough few weeks with a lot of travelling, suspensions, injuries and off-the-field comings and goings, seeing young players stepping in and doing a thoroughly professional job was a massive encouragement for the supporters.

I have learnt that the one thing fans won't tolerate is players who look as if they couldn't be bothered – those who lose the ball and don't chase back to win it again, and players that don't seem to be interested in chasing lost causes. The fans can stomach mistakes and failings if the attitude and commitment are there to seek to put it right. And maybe there is a lesson for life too – we may not always get it right, but have we got the right attitude, character and commitment to seek to put things right when we do get it wrong? How often do we adopt the 'can't be bothered' approach to dealing with life?

Arriving at the training ground that week, I anticipated that there would be a buzz and that the team would start to settle into a routine and pattern, but how wrong I was! Having had such a good few days with the draw against Luton and the win against York, it was only a matter of time before the unlucky streak that had been a feature of the 2010/11 season continued. This time it showed itself not only with Luke Berry's injury sustained against York, but in the recall of two players from their loan spells with Cambridge United.

There are in general terms two kinds of loans: firstly, the season-long loan, and secondly, the short-term loan, usually for 28 days. More often than not, once the 28 days is up, the loan can be extended if all parties agree, but there is normally a 24-hour recall option which means that the team the player is contracted to can call them back if they decide they need them.

AFC Wimbledon and Luton Town, because of injury and suspension, recalled Ricky Wellard and Dan Walker respectively, and both went straight back into their squads. And United had released Shaun Jeffers from his loan on the basis that he wasn't going to get games with the players who were around at that time. However, Courtney Herbert arrived on loan from Northampton Town.

Over the few weeks that Ricky had been with us, I had got chatting to him on a few occasions, but with no warning he was gone, as were Dan and Shaun. It reminded me again of how important it was to take the opportunities to speak with players, especially those in on loan.

It is probably true that over the six seasons I have been at United I have seen somewhere close to 200 players pass through the changing room doors, not including all the scholars. This season we will have had over 30 players by the end of the season, and that for a club with a small budget and a small squad.

At the last minute Tobias' visit to the club had to be cancelled as he wasn't well enough to come to the game. It was disappointing for all concerned. We spoke with the play team at Addenbrooke's Hospital about trying to get him along to another game before the end of the season.

The game we had selected for Tobias to attend was the last game of the month, the home game against Forest Green Rovers. As mentioned earlier, this would be our first meeting of the season with Forest Green Rovers in the league, as the previous week had also been our first encounter of the season with York City.

Continuing our 'Kick It Out' initiative, we joined up with the Level Playing Field campaign which seeks to address the issue of disability within football. Again Nick Parker led on this project, through which we welcomed some blind and partially sighted people to the game and had a specialised commentary for them. We hope that in the future this can become part of what the club offers, if we can find funds to purchase equipment and find and train volunteers to run the commentary.

The game was a frustrating one for United after the success of the games against Luton and York. United went ahead through Mark Bentley, but should have been out of sight before an equaliser from Forest Green rescued a point for them, the game ending 1–1.

There are times when a draw feels like a victory – perhaps a point has been earned when nothing was expected, as in our home match against Luton; or when, as in our home game against Tamworth, we were 3–0 down and got it back to 3–3. But there are other times when after the game the atmosphere created is like that of a defeat, and that was the case with this game. And it was compounded by the fact that Forest Green Rovers were one of the teams with us in and around the relegation zone – three points against them would have moved us further away from the danger of the drop.

It was hugely disappointing – there had been such expectation after Luton and York that we could get on a run and pull away. However, the frustration of the season continued.

Before kick-off, I was able to catch up with former United striker Liam Enver-Marum who, although he had travelled with the Forest Green team, had not been included in the 16-man squad. Liam had earlier in the season been back to the Abbey with Crawley and had subsequently been on loan to Hayes & Yeading (where he'd also played against the U's) before a January move to Forest Green. It had been a while since I'd had a chance to speak to him, but with him not involved there was time for a decent catch-up. There were two other ex-U's playing that day, although both were before my time at the Abbey.

The day before the Forest Green match I was at the ground to officiate at my first scattering of ashes on the pitch. The family who had contacted us back in November had finally managed to get everyone together for a date to come to the ground, and I met the family by the offices before leading them round to the pitch. Their request had been for their grandad's ashes to be scattered in the goal mouth at the Newmarket Road end, which Ian Darler had confirmed would be fine.

Over the years, I have had the privilege of leading ceremonies for the scattering and burial of ashes for families in people's garden's, in cemeteries and in a field! I had even written a ceremony that a family could use on a beach when they scattered the ashes in the sea. But this was my first at the club. It was an interesting experience for me – as I've said before about my approach to these kinds of occasions, I try to make them as personal and as accessible to everyone as I can, rather than seeing it as doing a job. The family seemed to appreciate the occasion, and hopefully Donald will have his name in the Book of Remembrance. Red roses were left in the goalmouth, to be removed before the warm-up the next day.

How many more opportunities there will be who knows? It was interesting that one of the directors stopped by as the ceremony was taking place and got chatting to Ian as he didn't realise it was something the club did.

Following a tour of the club that Greg and I had done earlier in the season with a men's group, one of the men had got in touch with me about running a tour for the team he was coach and manager for. He had first started with the team when they were under-8s and this was their final season as an under-16s team. He wanted there to be a really positive end to his involvement and hoped there would be an opportunity for them to hear something about his faith.

So Greg and I welcomed the parents and players from the Bottisham Colts Under-16s football team (around 35 people in all) to the Abbey the Friday night before the Forest Green Rovers match. At my suggestion they had been for a curry first, and had wandered over for the tour. Because of the numbers we split into two groups after an initial welcome and chat in the home dressing room. Greg took a group into the physio room, while I took a group through hospitality, the boardroom, the referees' room and then we swapped over. Both groups ended in the away dressing room where we finished the tour.

As we had discovered that not everyone knew that we were Christians and therefore weren't expecting a talk at the end of the tour, I simply wrapped up the evening by sharing a little of how and why I got involved in the football club as chaplain, and what a club like Cambridge United are doing with their very own 'vicar'! It wasn't a heavy ending, pitched at a comfortable level without anyone feeling we were taking advantage of the situation to give a quick sell for the Christian faith. Greg and I are both very sensitive to that issue and felt this was at an appropriate level. It did stir up a few questions. Some of the group came back for the Forest Green game, met a couple of the injured players at half-time to ask them some questions, and at the end had their photo taken with one of the players. This would be the last tour of the season – although there was interest in running a further tour, Greg and I felt it appropriate to hold off till the new season.

So the penultimate month of the 2010/11 season ended with the U's having played 6, lost 1, won 1 and drawn 4, giving season-to-date statistics of: played 40, won 10, drawn 14, lost 16 on 44 points. The month ended with them sitting in 16th place, and moving into the last month of the season, with six games to go, they were still some way from securing their place in the Conference Premier for the 2011/12 season.

It was proving to be a tense few weeks, and whereas in some seasons the magic 40 points would have seen you home and dry, that clearly wasn't going to be the case this season – exactly how many points would see the U's safe was a matter of opinion. Jez and the players, along with the supporters, were desperate to secure safety rather than having to depend on the results of the teams around us.

March Results

Tues 1	Blue Square Bet Premier	**Newport County 1 United 1**
		Russell
Sat 5	Blue Square Bet Premier	**Darlington 1 United 0**
Sat 12	Blue Square Bet Premier	**Southport 1 United 1**
		Berry
Tues 15	Blue Square Bet Premier	**United 0 Luton Town 0**
Sat 19	Blue Square Bet Premier	**United 2 York City 1**
		Hughes, Wright
Sat 26	Blue Square Bet Premier	**United 1 Forest Green Rovers 1**
		Bentley

April 2011

A further addition to the playing squad arrived in the final month of the 2010/11 season. Dean Sinclair joined the U's on loan from Grimsby until the end of the season. He had scored against us in the 1–1 draw at Blundell Park in February, but had fallen out of favour there, and so Jez brought him in, as it was anticipated that Luke Berry would be out for the rest of the season with his ankle injury.

Dean made his debut in another relegation six-pointer away at Altrincham at the start of the month. Goals from Brian Saah and Liam Hughes rescued a point for the U's, with United having fallen behind by two goals in the first period.

The point kept United in 16th place, but two draws in two games against teams that were below them meant that United were not yet free of the threat of relegation – victories against them both would have secured their place next season. As it was, it looked likely that it was going to go down to the wire, with United still needing to pick up valuable points.

Looking at the teams around us in the relegation battle, I felt that we were one of the stronger sides in there and should, on paper at least, be able to pull away. But as had been the case all season, it only took a decision to go against us, an injury to be picked up, or one mistake, and suddenly the whole thing could turn on its head.

So much was riding on surviving in the Blue Square Bet Premier – no decisions could be taken by anyone at the club because no one knew what the new season would look like. It was business as usual, but with a certain added pressure.

It took me back to the 2006/07 season, my second at the club, when Jimmy Quinn had come in as manager part-way through the season, replacing Rob Newman. On the last day of that season, any one of six teams could have filled the final relegation place. United faced a home encounter with Tamworth, who had already been relegated. A Robbie Simpson goal gave the U's a 1–0 victory. And as it happened, Altrincham, who finished in the fourth relegation place, were subsequently given a stay of execution as Boston United dropped straight from the Football League to the Conference North.

I could still remember the heart-in-mouth feelings of that last game of that season and the atmosphere around the club in the lead up to it, and it was not something I wanted any of us to go through again. Looking at the fixtures still to come through April, I was desperately hoping it wouldn't go down to the final game again this year.

At times like this, the role of chaplain is an interesting one because you are there to be someone players and fans can turn to. And yet in my situation, and I can't speak for other chaplains, I feel the loss as much as the next fan does. While outwardly there is a job to do to help people process what they are experiencing and going through, inwardly I am often feeling the same emotions and frustrations. I remember, for example, after our second defeat at Wembley in the play-off finals against Torquay, talking with one of the fans the next day back at the club. He had felt really low and had thought about ringing me to have a chat, because he somehow felt it would help him feel better. I didn't tell him that I felt exactly the same way!

Every season, up and down the country, there are chaplains who experience the euphoria of promotions, cup victories, play-off final wins; and yet there are also chaplains who experience relegation, cup final defeats, and as I know all too well, play-off final losses. Having a chaplain doesn't somehow make you immune from these difficult and painful moments. Chaplaincy isn't a ticket to success. The chaplain is there for the good times and the bad; the joys and elation of victory as well as the disappointment of defeat. In my case, I live and feel those emotions. At the same time, I believe there is more to life than a football result, and a hope which is not dependent on a refereeing decision or the width of the woodwork.

And this is the challenge I face being a Baptist minister and chaplain – I must seek to be real, while at the same time still being able to offer help and hope to those who need it. There is no use me pretending that everything is hunky-dory, that I never struggle or feel low, that I don't have really tough days and days where I wonder how I'm going to get through. At the same time, I must ensure that I deal appropriately with how I feel if I'm going to be able to help others.

And perhaps this is where the Church has been weak in the past, and perhaps even in some areas still is today. The church I grew up in had many strengths, but one of its weaknesses to my mind was that it wasn't a place where you could talk about feelings or emotions; it wasn't a place that created the space to be able to work through challenges and difficulties. The Church has perhaps at one extreme alienated people with a sense of unreality – it hasn't been the place to talk about struggles, and everything has seemed black and white – although not in the world I live in! At the other extreme, the Church has perhaps at times left people without hope. One survey, conducted by a church in the USA, asked local people why they didn't go to church: the second most popular response was 'I've got enough problems of my own; why would I go to church? If the Church can't fix its own problems, how on earth are they going to be able to fix mine?'

It is my view that what the world needs from the Church is a healthy dose of reality, seasoned with the hope that comes from faith in Jesus Christ. And when that does happen, the Christian faith and the Church become suddenly so much more attractive as a place that people can come to, with their hang-ups and struggles, and find there to be others who are also struggling. But people can also find hope there, even in the seemingly blackest of holes.

We welcomed back the recently departed Ricky Wellard with his AFC Wimbledon team-mates for United's next home game. Ricky received a very warm reception from the home fans when introduced. Ricky had walked back into the Wimbledon team and had been putting in some really good performances – this was one of those situations where the loan spell had worked to the player's advantage.

Wimbledon were a very good side – they kept the ball well and moved it around, and United did well to keep them to just two goals. And then Danny Wright popped up with a goal with eight minutes to go, making for a frantic final few minutes.

Wimbledon held out for a win, 2–1, but the score didn't really tell the tale. United did have their chances, but Wimbledon were a class act, many saying they were the best team to have visited the Abbey all season. We had come up against a very good side, who for large parts of the game had outplayed us. However, at the final reckoning, we hadn't been that far away – we had hung in there, got a goal back and could so easily, on another afternoon, have taken something from the game.

After the game, I was able to catch up with Ricky briefly before he jumped on the team coach. He wished us well for the rest of the season, and I likewise wished him and Wimbledon well.

There were just four games to go, and it was all so very tight at the bottom of the table, with seven teams separated by five points, from Barrow in 16th to Altrincham in 22nd. United were lying in 17th place, with the pressure cranked up just a little bit more.

Arriving at training always carries a sense of the unknown about it – will the players be there? What will they be doing? Will the scholars be there too? Will there be anyone new around? What opportunities will there be for conversation? Sometimes, as has been seen over the season thus far, there is disappointment – I arrive to find no one there. At other times, there are unexpected bonuses. At training during April, there was more of the second than the first, which was great for me, and the weather was fantastic, which always helps!

On this particular occasion, Renford Sargeant, one of the club directors, was at training, which gave me the opportunity to stand with him watching the lads train, while talking to him a little about his business and how he got involved with United. My contact with Renford to this point had largely been on match days, and more often than not, our longer conversations had been at away games. But here I was presented with an opportunity to talk a little about my work outside of the club, and hopefully for Renford to understand a little bit more about my role.

And over the six seasons I have been involved at the club, I have been amazed at the significant moments, opportunities and conversations that have taken place and in some cases perhaps kept doors opened that may have been closed, or opened others. I have been privileged to be asked to take the funerals of a number of folk connected to the club – relatives of directors and staff, along with some fans – and these moments have not only provided an opportunity for me to highlight the value of the role, but also to get a little closer to the staff and directors.

I do believe that God works through all things and many significant conversations have come as a result of praying for the club, the people and my work there. I believe that here I had received another God-given opportunity to spend a few moments with one of the senior club directors.

I also noticed that there was a new young lad playing in goal. After training over lunch, I had the opportunity to find out that he was Andrew Plummer, who had originally been with Ipswich Town in their academy (along with Darryl Coakley) before moving to Northern Ireland to play first for Bangor, then for Glenavon. In his last game for them he had been sent off, and as the season was drawing to a close he wouldn't be featuring in any more of their games. Come the end of the season, he was looking for a move back to England and as Cambridge was close to his family base in Ipswich, he asked if he could come along and train with them. As I've mentioned previously, this does happen from time to time – players wanting to keep training while at the same time looking for a club.

It reminded me again that my work as chaplain extends beyond Cambridge United. Who knows where Andrew will end up playing? But my hope and prayer is that the few minutes he had with the chaplain of Cambridge United that day will have left a positive impression. It struck me again that this is also true of my wider role within the church, and it reminded me of a quote I read recently by Mark Hope-Urwin, the Head of Hospitality at Birmingham Cathedral, who said, 'You have five seconds to make an impression, be it good or bad.' If that is true then everything I do counts, every conversation, every smile, every handshake … whether that be on the training ground, in the boardroom, in the stands with one of the stewards, in hospital visiting, or at the school, as well as in church.

The scholars were also there that day; some of the senior scholars were involved with the first team training, while the first years were involved in a 'behind closed doors' game against a Histon youth team in the afternoon. It soon became obvious that some of the second years who hadn't been offered a development contract had left already, having finished their college work. From my perspective this is always hard – from having had contact through hosting them at our home, watching them occasionally, and seeing them at training, for them to be gone with no opportunity to shake their hands and wish them well is tough. Occasionally, I do manage to get a phone number so I can drop them a text, but with the scholars that is not common. It is one of those areas that I look at each year and wonder how I can improve my role in this.

One of the significant changes that had happened over the last season was that the players now had lunch together at the training ground after training. With Martin Ling the players were required to provide their own lunch, and now under Jez, a big pan of pasta served with sauce, beans, tuna and/or toast was the order of the day. With players travelling from a variety of distances, this had become a key time to help build team spirit.

From my perspective it did mean the players were around a little longer after training and this did open up opportunities to chat to them and join in with a bit of banter. For the majority of the last few months of the season, the banter had been spared for Millsy, who as he had been unable to join in training had acted as chef. He had risen to this challenge – he does like to keep a tidy kitchen, which is just as well as Robbie Nightingale was usually around keeping an eye on things!

On the SCORE network an email arrived from Steve Prince, the chaplain at Reading FC. They were holding an opening ceremony for their Garden of Remembrance. This acted as a timely reminder that we hadn't yet held our official opening for the Memorial Garden, which had now finally been finished.

So I arranged with Ian Darler, Will Jones and Claudine Bone to hold this before the home game against Hayes & Yeading on Easter Saturday. I contacted Steve and obtained a copy of the order of service that he had put together and the words that had been used.

We then made contact with the suppliers who had helped with donations to make the garden what it was – Ivett & Reed, local stonemasons for the memorial stone and Ridgeons Timber and Builders Merchants who had supplied paving slabs, sand and cement. I contacted Jeremy Sallis at BBC Radio Cambridgeshire to ask if he would be willing to come and officially open the garden. Through Claudine we arranged for two places in hospitality for each as a thank you.

I took the order of service Steve had used at Reading and personalised it to our situation at Cambridge and then added in logos to produce a service sheet. I was invited by Jeremy to do a radio interview on Good Friday morning to talk about the Memorial Garden and the Book of Remembrance. One of the fans who is a graphic designer had agreed to design our leaflet for the Book of Remembrance – things were falling into place.

The service itself was attended by about 20 people – folk who had helped to develop the Memorial Garden, and some who had some connection to the garden, mainly through the wall that had been created from dedications that had been submitted, as well as club representatives.

To be honest, in some ways the short service felt a little contrived, but nonetheless I felt it important to mark the culmination of the work on this garden. I do believe in the relevance of sacred spaces – places that people can go to find some space to think, to reflect and to ponder. Our world is so full of busyness that these spaces are hard to come by and yet as human beings we need them. It is my hope and prayer that this Memorial Garden may become a sacred space at the club, and out of it there may come more opportunities to share with folk in the questions that they have.

For United's penultimate away game, we took a trip to Gloucestershire to play Forest Green Rovers. This was definitely a game that we could not afford to lose – a draw would suffice, but a win would be great.

Luke Berry had made a remarkable recovery from his ankle injury, had taken to the field against Wimbledon and took his place again against Forest Green. Thirteen minutes into the game, he bravely went in for a header and there was a clash of heads which knocked Luke out and required him to be stretchered off to hospital, where he ended up with six staples in his scalp.

Luke was replaced by Dean Sinclair, who scored for the U's in first-half stoppage time. However, the U's again committed the cardinal sin of immediately conceding a goal, and before the end of first-half stoppage time, Forest Green were level. The second half was played out and the game ended in a 1–1 draw. There were thoughts of what could have been if only we had hung on and frustration for Luke's sake, and the season's bad fortune seemingly continued to haunt the U's. Fortunately, Luke was discharged that evening and he and Greg Reid caught up with the coach on the way back to Cambridge.

Our penultimate home game was against Hayes & Yeading and took place on Easter Saturday on a blazing hot afternoon, with temperatures soaring to the high twenties. Amazingly, Luke Berry was back again and in the starting line up, although sporting a rugby-style scrum hat – just what you'd want in that heat. It showed the character of this young man though – at the age of just 18, he had bounced back from an ankle injury that had been predicted to keep him out for the rest of the season after a couple of weeks, and then a week after being knocked out, with the staples still in, he took the field again. It was tangible evidence of the work that Jez and Nolan had been doing with the players – this was the kind of resilience and character that the team needed if they were to survive.

And how much was that needed on that afternoon, after James Jennings received a straight red card for a robust but not vicious tackle on 23 minutes. I actually missed seeing this as it happened, as I had been in the medical room – one of the Hayes & Yeading players had a cut above his eye that needed a couple of stitches. The tackle by James Jennings happened as I was on my way back over to the stand.

I decided to make my way to the dressing room to see Jenno. It isn't something I do every time a player is sent off, but it was a decision I took on the day. While there with James, we were joined by Sam Ives, who had been sacrificed as the pack was shuffled to accommodate the situation. Sam was equally frustrated – he had not had many opportunities and this was one of only a handful of starts he had had. He was gutted to be taken off, especially as his contract was up at the end of the season. What he needed was games to be able to prove he was worthy of a new contract, but because of the misfortune of another, his chance had gone.

The U's held on and defended resolutely, and with ten minutes to go Jordan Patrick got on the end of a Conal Platt cross to put the ball in the net and send the crowd into a frenzy for a moment, until they realised that they needed to hang on for a few more minutes, as the match was extended by a further five minutes of added time. But hold out the U's did, claiming a well-deserved 1–0 win, and all but securing survival for another season.

Mathematically it was still possible for the U's to get caught if results went against us and our goal difference was overturned by ten goals over the remaining two games of the season. But at the end of the day the win was a magnificent achievement under difficult conditions.

For the past three seasons I have got into the habit of taking my eldest three boys, Kieran, Curtis and Jordan, to the last away game of the season. When the fixtures come out at the start of the season, one of the first things they look for now is who the last away game of the season is. For some reason, we always manage to bag a long trip – over the past three seasons we've travelled to Northwich Victoria, Salisbury City and Altrincham, and this season it was the turn of York City.

We normally stand on the terraces with the United fans. Last season at Altrincham, as I knew the Altrincham chaplain, Andy Barclay-Watt, I met up with him and he took me to the dressing room to see the players before the game. This season, through club secretary, Lisa Baldwin, contacting her counterpart at York City, I was able to get to see the players in the dressing room and pitchside before the game, and meet up with them afterwards before setting off back to Cambridge.

I had contacted the York City chaplain, Chris Cullwick as we had met at the chaplains' conference and swapped emails over the years, but never managed to make it to each other's grounds. However, he was away and contacted me on his return from holiday to let me know he'd missed it. York City also have a patron, the Most Reverend and Right Honourable Dr John Sentamu, Archbishop of York, who I had the pleasure of sharing lunch with the previous October. He is very down-to-earth and we had a little Cambridge United/York City banter over lunch. But he wasn't at the game either, sadly.

The game itself was another good battling performance from United, holding out for a 0–0 draw and confirmation that they would be playing Conference Premier football again in 2011/12.

Following the news that the club had been put up for sale, it became obvious that cuts would be required to staffing levels, and at that point Lisa Baldwin gave notice that she would leave as club secretary at the end of the season. I had spoken to Lisa about her decision when the news first broke. Robert Smith also gave notice that he would step down as general manager at the same time. For both of them, their last game would be the Fleetwood Town game on the last day of April, and their last official office day would be the Thursday, with the Royal Wedding Bank Holiday on the Friday. And then some while later, Will Jones tendered his resignation as PR, marketing and media manager at the same time, also finishing at the end of April.

As has been mentioned throughout the season, change is tough and can be unsettling. Of course, it can be good too and often is necessary. But as I reflect on my role at the club over six seasons and the many changes in staffing I have experienced, each change has slightly altered the working relationship, and in particular who I need to relate to for different aspects of my work.

With my pitchside duties, I have had three different people in the few years I have needed to link up with. When it comes to pastoral matters, such as the information flow about deaths of fans, this has improved in the past season, but who will pick that up next season is not clear. However, although the questions are there, the answers won't come just yet, and I'll need to pick that up once the season has finished and the dust begins to settle again.

It was another tangible reminder of how much we can take people and relationships for granted. It also made me realise again how change can be not just disruptive but also unsettling. There were many questions I had about my role and how it would develop over the close season and into the 2011/12 season, but it was too early for answers.

Our last game of the season was a home fixture against Fleetwood Town. Due to the live televising of one of the Conference Premier matches, all games in the league kicked off at the same time – 5.15 p.m.

By the last game of the season all matters at the top end of the table had been resolved, play-off places had been secured and no one in the top five could be caught by anyone else, so there was nothing further to play for except taking confidence and form into the play-off semi-finals. The only matter to be resolved was who would be relegated, with any two from five (Barrow, Forest Green Rovers, Southport, Tamworth and Altrincham) joining Eastbourne Borough and Histon.

The game itself was a largely forgettable affair, Fleetwood opting to play a second string team with one eye on the play-off semi-finals. United dominated much of the game in terms of possession but didn't take the chances they created and conceded a sloppy goal late in the second half. It appeared that the exertion of the previous weekend had still not got out of their systems, and it summed up the season.

Former United frontman, Magno Vieira, who had last played for United in the first play-off final defeat to Exeter City, and was Fleetwood's leading scorer for the season, played the first 45 minutes. It was good to see yet another former player back at United, and I was able to wish him well for the play-offs before he left for the long trip back north.

From a playing perspective it hadn't been a great ending to the season; it felt a little flat after the scenes the previous weekend following the win over Hayes & Yeading and the three points that all but ensured United wouldn't be scrapping on the last day of the season for survival. However, following the final whistle, we were able to conduct presentations on the pitch for the player of the season awards.

Because of Will's impending departure, and the fact that he finished on the Thursday before the last home game, he had asked if I would organise and coordinate the club's player of the year awards. In the previous few seasons, it had been my privilege to host these as part of my match-day responsibilities. They had taken place in the small window between the players' warm-up and leaving the pitch to get ready for the game.

Liaising with Jez ahead of that final game, he requested that we conducted the presentations after the final whistle. I had a long chat with him about this and about the pattern of that last game and what happened afterwards. With the later kick-off, by the time we reached the end of the game, the scholars had returned from their game as CRC, and Jez was keen to include them in the presentations. He also wanted to introduce the new intake of scholars, who would be the new first years come pre-season.

So following that final whistle, the man of the match presentations, which usually take place in the hospitality area, took place on the pitch. We introduced the CRC team and the new intake of scholars before carrying out the various player of the season awards. It provided a positive note to end the season, following the disappointment of the game itself.

And so the season ended, with United's league record showing: played 46, won 11, drawn 17, lost 18, with 50 points and finishing 17th. While things on the pitch had finished for the season there was still work to do. There was the small matter of deciding on the management for the new season, and players' contracts to be resolved … even though there was no more football, there was still much to do.

April Results

Sat 2	Blue Square Bet Premier	**Altrincham 2 United 2** *Saah, Hughes*
Sat 9	Blue Square Bet Premier	**United 1 AFC Wimbledon 2** *Wright*
Sat 16	Blue Square Bet Premier	**Forest Green Rovers 1 United 1** *Sinclair*
Sat 23	Blue Square Bet Premier	**United 1 Hayes & Yeading 0** *Patrick*
Mon 25	Blue Square Bet Premier	**York City 0 United 0**
Sat 30	Blue Square Bet Premier	**United 0 Fleetwood Town 1**

May 2011

At the start of the season, there had been a quiet confidence around the club – an expectation that the new lads who had been brought in, together with the existing squad of players, would be able to push United on from the 10th placed finish of the 2009/10 campaign. The hope had been that by the end of the season we would be in and around the play-off places.

As the season progressed and players were injured, the goals didn't come as hoped, performances dropped below par, decisions went against us and mistakes cost goals, so the level of expectation dropped and by mid-season, although there was still the outside possibility of being in and around the play-off places, a finish akin to the previous season would have been acceptable.

The home form wasn't as good as the away form, and Martin Ling seemed not to have had his fair share of the breaks – he appeared to be on the receiving end of some poor decisions and bad luck on the pitch which ended with his contract being terminated at the beginning of February. The club, being in a financially challenging position, had appointed a caretaker manager from within, and the last few weeks of the season had caused a fair amount of nervousness. There had at the same time been some positive things to take away from the season, with Liam Hughes and Luke Berry emerging from the CRC team to make positive contributions to the first team and give hope that they would push on next season.

As the season draws to a close and the on-field matters get resolved, there is a fair amount of reflection that takes place – what went wrong and right, what needs to change, who needs to be released, where do we need to strengthen, how can we make savings while not jeopardising the club's future? All these issues are thought through in those weeks towards the end of the season and just after.

In the immediate aftermath of the season, I spent a bit of time with various staff members talking over what was next for them in their respective roles, reflecting back on the challenges of the previous season and talking about their hopes and fears for the new season. With significant changes and a reduction in the number of office staff, there were naturally a few matters needing to be resolved – and not just who would be in which office! While at the York match, I had spoken to Julie Ankers and Nigel Ashman as we stood on the terraces and had had the opportunity to hear from them about their priorities for the close season, and how they felt things would improve or not. Being in a position to listen was a privilege and I hoped it was of some value to the staff too.

I'm not sure how it works at other clubs, but at Cambridge United it has been my experience that players being released and not being offered new contracts are usually told at the end of the season, and so early in May the decision was taken to not offer new contracts to Sam Ives, Darryl Coakley or Dave Partridge. The loan players also returned to their parent clubs and so there was a little exodus of players – at this stage less than in the previous seasons while I had been at the club. I dropped text messages to the three United players that had been released as I didn't have the opportunity to see them, wishing them well for the future.

The decision as to who would be the next manager at the club was yet to be made – various names had been mentioned, but as a result of the financial constraints the club was under, it became obvious that Jez George was the board's favourite candidate. It was his to accept or decline, but he also recognised the position the club was in. The effect on the youth scheme was his major concern and once this was resolved, he agreed to take the post, with Nolan as his number two and coach.

Once that decision was taken, Jez had the task of working out his playing squad for the new season within the revised budget he had been given. This had been significantly reduced from that of the previous campaign, mainly due to the attendances being lower during the 2010/11 season than forecast. Having released three players, Jez offered development contracts to Luke Allen and James Brighton, joining Jonathan Thorpe who had already signed a development contract, all three having finished their two-year scholarships. He also offered a further year to Jack Eades. Jordan Patrick,

Liam Hughes and Luke Berry all signed professional contracts for one, two and three years respectively.

This new strategy had been introduced by Jez a couple of years previously. With the development contract the players were registered to play for both CRC and Cambridge United, whereas with the pro contract they were only registered to play for the first team, and if they needed to play for CRC this had to be done via a loan between the two teams. This had occurred a couple of times in previous seasons, when players who were recovering from longer-term injury had been given a 28-day loan to CRC to gain match fitness.

The development contracts also offer players who have shown potential, but perhaps have not quite done enough to earn a pro contract, the opportunity to be kept at the club a little bit longer to see how they progress. Prior to the introduction of this contract, the manager would have to decide at the end of the two-year scholarship whether to offer a pro contract or not. The other significant issue which made this such an attractive option was that the cost of the development contracts was funded through the youth scheme and not out of the manager's playing budget. In this way, players could be kept on for a further year or two to see whether they did enough to justify a pro contract. It has been a very advantageous move for all concerned, and through the previous couple of seasons a number of players had come through this scheme and made it into the first team, players that without the offer of a development contract would not still have been with United.

The close season always provides for some movement of players at all levels of the game. At some clubs this movement is greater than at others, and I have had seasons where there has been a significant turnover and others where the turnover has been less.

There have been some seasons where I have been at the club as players have been told whether they were being offered a renewed contract or were being released, and in that moment, to be able to shake the hands of those leaving and wish them well has been a privilege. At other times the players have been called in over different days and so it simply hasn't been possible to be at the club for the whole duration of these conversations. In those cases, a text message has been the next best thing.

This particular close season there was an additional challenge for Jez – the matter of having to work within a reduced playing budget, which amongst other things meant that a new wage structure would need to be introduced. It was likely that some players still under contract would be encouraged either to find another club or to take a reduction in wages.

For some of the players with families to support, these were not easy times and it was hard to know which way to go. With financial pressures hitting many clubs, it wasn't just Cambridge United that had to cut its playing budget and squad size, which meant fewer opportunities to find new clubs at a similar level.

As chaplain, I am not party to these decisions, and often the way I find out about players signing or being released is like everyone else – through the club website or local media. Very occasionally over the seasons, I have happened to be at the club when a player has been there either to sign or to be released, but that is more fortuitous than planned. And so it is that with the arrival of new players I need to wait until pre-season to meet them, and for players being released or moving on, the text message has to be the way to send them my best wishes.

Through the month, it was clear from what was reported and statements released by the club that negotiations were ongoing with some of the senior players to seek to cut the wage bill, and at the same time work was being done to strengthen the squad, with Tom Shaw arriving from Kidderminster, Michael Wylde from Tamworth, and the promise of more as the summer carried on. Kevin Roberts had agreed a further year's contract, while Simon Russell was considering his situation, having within his contract an option to extend it for a further year.

Changes would still be made to the playing squad before pre-season and also during pre-season. For most players, contracts run from July to June; and it is often the case that players won't be signed until pre-season kicks off. With playing squads being cut across all leagues, this time round there would be a good number of players available and some of these would be invited to join in pre-season at clubs before a decision was taken to offer them a contract or not, to see how they fit in to the squad as well as to assess their fitness and ability.

While Jez and Nolan were concentrating on the first team squad, they also had an eye on the new youth intake. The club has Centre of Excellence teams from under-9s right the way through to under-16s. Of all the players involved in these squads, one or two may be offered a scholarship, Luke Berry being the most recent player to come through the ranks.

The club is always looking for new talent and players that have potential. As the season ended, a series of football tournaments and trial games were held with a place in one of the Centre of Excellence or development squads as the possible reward, while for others the offer of a CRC contract or even a pro-contract might be there if they performed well enough.

The difference between the Centre of Excellence and development squads is that at the Centre of Excellence the lads will be playing for Cambridge United at the relevant age groups as well as training together twice during the week. The development squads are a tier below this, and the lads will be playing for their mini-league or colts teams and training once a week with a CUFC coach. They will also be playing in games during the holidays against other local professional teams or the Centre of Excellence teams, with the view to some of these players progressing through to the Centre of Excellence teams. There are also 18 regional centres across mid-Anglia which offer weekly training sessions and friendly fixtures, with the aim of feeding players into both the development and Centre of Excellence squads.

I went along one Friday early in May to watch the last trial game. It was a behind closed doors game on the Abbey pitch, and although there were relatively few people around, being there I was able to spend a bit of time chatting with Ian Darler and James Wynne, and at the end caught up with Jez and Nolan. There were a couple of faces I recognised in the game itself, and who we will see back at the Abbey, if anyone, remains to be seen.

Was I required to be present at the game itself? No. But my experience has been that putting myself into these kinds of situations provides opportunities for talking to folk in ways that don't often happen on match days. It is also a practical outworking of my approach to my role at the club – deliberately making myself available and accessible.

The Smile Scheme had been a success through the 2010/11 season, although there was still room for improvement. One of the ideas that I had been working on with Marshall Ford was for a more permanent Smile Scheme board that could be placed in various locations around the ground, where literature for the charities could be displayed and the running total raised for the season updated match by match. While this had been published in the match-day programme and I had mentioned it from pitchside, not everyone got the message and there had been nowhere for literature to be displayed. It was also planned to create a short weekly web article about the charity of the day, and I managed to find someone who was prepared to do this for the club each week.

The one disappointment from the season with regard to the Smile Scheme had been the lack of take-up for the free seats. These had been offered to people connected with the nominated charity of the day alongside the collections, and while for some games the demand had been there, for other games and other charities they were more interested in having the collection than in promoting the free seats to the games. This is an area we need to address as we look ahead.

There were still some loose ends to tie together – producing a photograph montage of the various groups and presentations during the season, a further press release, and having a review meeting had all been talked about but needed to be actioned. Clearly there was a way to go in developing the scheme, although good progress had been made and over £7,500 had been raised for both local and national charities over the course of the 2010/11 season.

Occasionally, there will be a link created through the chaplaincy work that will continue and grow beyond my role. One player that I have had regular contact with over the years is Andy Duncan. Andy played for United for nine seasons, moving down from Manchester United. After finishing his professional playing career at United he remained on the staff in the commercial department for a season.

Andy has become a friend and we meet regularly for a coffee and catch up. It is a thrill for me when years down the line there remains still that contact and friendship.

Another player who has left United that I still have some contact with is Dan Gleeson and I managed to catch up with Dan ahead of Luton's play-off final game against AFC Wimbledon at the City of Manchester stadium. Unfortunately for Dan, this ended up being his third play-off final defeat, having been involved with both finals United played and lost, with Luton losing to AFC Wimbledon on penalties. And I've mentioned already that Greg Reid, who I first met in December 2004, has become a good friend and has been a real support in my work at the club and beyond. It is a thrill to have Greg and his wife Trudy at the church with us now.

There are other friendships that have grown out of the contact that I have had at the club, and in my role I am always keen to look for further opportunities that might develop and how I can become more than just a chaplain and establish a friendship.

It remains one of the great challenges for all chaplains – the relationship between club and church or other work. There are some in our churches who will turn their backs on chaplaincy because they cannot see a clear link between the two. Is it essential that there is a clear link, or not? I can only reflect on my own experience. There have been times over the six seasons when my involvement at the football club as chaplain has been questioned – particularly in the early days. Latterly, Barnwell have been very supportive and see the value of my involvement.

In reality, many players travel to the club, and so even if they did want to explore the Christian faith, our church wouldn't be the obvious one at which to do it. And for a club like Cambridge United, a large proportion of the fans travel in to the games from the surrounding areas too – Ely, St Ives, Saffron Walden, Bury St Edmunds to name but a few of the town hubs that provide many of our loyal fans. There is also a handful who will travel much further distances. Will these folk end up at Barnwell? It is very unlikely.

But Barnwell Baptist Church understands that by releasing me to serve the club, in a small way, the Christian message is being shared with an audience that would not normally darken the doors of the church. But more than that, the church is demonstrating that it is still relevant and has something to offer in our very post-Christian world.

With the pressure off as regards fixtures, there was a little more time to chat about things other than football with the staff, and on one visit I had a conversation with Claudine, who was asking about the church at Barnwell and how it worked. It was helpful to be reminded that for many people their experience of church is very different from how some churches are today – and the way Barnwell works is quite different from the traditional view of what church is and how it operates.

Her memories of church and how she described them to me, while I could relate to them, did not equate to how we do things at Barnwell. I invited her along one week to see what it was like, but as she is not a local resident, it is very difficult to see how that will happen. Again, it highlighted the challenge and perhaps the conflict between the local church and the chaplaincy role.

But it isn't just hard to reconcile church and club – there is also the fact that I find it hard personally too, when relationships have been established with players, managers and staff who then move on to new places. As I've described, very often there is no opportunity for closure to the relationship, except by text. So I value even more those contacts that do remain after Cambridge United and that extend beyond the role of chaplain.

I, and the church at Barnwell, fully accept that in my role, while there is a close geographical link between the club and the church, and we have seen a handful of people begin to attend the church as a result of my work with the club, the reality is that the church is unlikely to see large numbers start attending because of the work. But there is a willingness to engage with the opportunities that arise at the club, and hopefully to build some lasting friendships that will go beyond the club and geographical boundaries. The value of chaplaincy must not be measured by the age-old 'bums on seats' yardstick. For any considering the opportunity to serve in chaplaincy there has to be another way to measure its value, if such a thing is needed. For me, as I've said many times over the season, I am truly grateful for a supportive church who do not demand that I produce facts and figures to justify my work, but willingly release me to this ministry.

The second Cambridge Homeless World Cup took place one Sunday afternoon in May. Speaking with Nigel Ashman in the lead-up to this event, I discovered that the plan to have some of the coaches getting involved with the teams and running some coaching with them had fallen in to place, and on the day, the coaches served as referees for the various games that were played.

I went along to catch the end of the afternoon, to show my face and to offer my support to Nigel and the coaches, and also to meet up again with Mike Smith, the organiser. It was a hot afternoon, and the teams each played a number of games in leagues before the final round of matches took place, the final being between Wintercomfort and the winners of the first tournament in 2010, the YMCA. The two teams couldn't be separated during the final, or during extra time, so it came down to the dreaded penalty shoot out. Wintercomfort took the title and the trophy was presented by the previous year's player of the tournament, Musa Kamara.

There was also an opportunity to invite the winning team to United so that we could present the trophy and medals on the pitch, while at the same time acknowledging the club's involvement through the Youth and Community Trust.

The organisers had been very pleased with the way the club had supported the tournament, and it had also provided an opportunity for Nigel to have conversations about other ways in which the trust could get involved with these groups throughout the year. Nigel was hopeful that an ongoing relationship would be established. As is often the case, once a contact and link has been established, it can open doors and as the trust seeks to become more involved in the community, involvement in these events is very welcome and also very necessary.

I had two further speaking engagements during the month – both for Christian football clubs at their end-of-season awards evenings. The first was for the Cambridge-based Ambassadors Football Club, where I was asked to talk a little about my work as chaplain, share a story or two, and share a little of my faith and how it related to football. The second was in Bury St Edmunds, where I was invited to return to the team I used to play for, Sporting '87 and to share in a similar way.

I am aware that being a chaplain does create an opportunity to talk about faith and football, to write a book, to tell a story, and while not unique around the country, there aren't many sports chaplains in the Cambridge area. It is a privilege I have and take seriously – I take any opportunity I can have to share my faith – although I need to be careful with how much I take on beyond the church.

It had not been possible to bring Tobias along to a game in the season – the two matches we had tried for had not worked out. So we hadn't yet had a chance to give him the goody bag we had put together for him, including his signed shirt. I arranged with Josh Coulson to visit Tobias one day in hospital and to deliver his gifts.

Although he was pleased to see them, he was very sleepy and it was a struggle for him to keep his eyes open. But to see the big smile when he saw his shirt was a privilege. We spoke to the play nurses about seeing whether we could arrange something for either pre-season or the start of the new season and so we left hopeful that he may get along to watch the lads sometime.

Josh and I grabbed a coffee and had a catch-up – Josh had just returned from being with the England C team, and had got his first cap coming on as a second-half substitute. It also gave me the opportunity to chat to him about his time at United, his hopes and aspirations for the future and how the family were doing.

He told me that the lads who were not on holiday were in for a fitness session the next day, which gave me the opportunity to catch up with those there. One or two had been away and so it was good to hear their news and stories.

As soon as the season is over and games have finished on the pitch, Ian and Mick, along with their team of helpers get to work on the playing surface. As has been highlighted already, the pitch at United is second to none in this league and is of a better quality than many of the pitches at league clubs. The work required has to be squeezed in to a very tight schedule and often with a very tight budget. Unlike at other clubs, there aren't the resources to re-lay the pitch every close season. And one thing that you can be sure of is that come the first home game of pre-season, the pitch will look magnificent.

Popping by the club to see these guys is one of the things I enjoy – they are all very down to earth men, but I have been privileged to support them through some pretty difficult times. Towards the end of the season, one of the volunteers lost his wife to cancer and I was able to take the funeral service of a grandmother-in-law of another. They are genuinely appreciative of the support they receive and while I do receive my fair share of banter (usually about the weather and my prayer life), it is a privilege to be a friend to these guys.

Ian had spoken to me during the season about trying to increase the use of the newly refurbished hospitality areas. The particular idea he had was to approach a funeral director with the view to wakes being held at the club. As I had the contacts locally, I managed to set a meeting up between a local firm and Ian, Claudine and myself. It was a very positive time and will hopefully bring more use for the hospitality at the club, which largely stands empty during the week. Being able to use the contacts I have to benefit the club is something I have been keen to do from the start, and may have become apparent through the stories of this past season.

This past season has been eventful – there have been some highs, there have perhaps been more lows; there have been a number of 'firsts' for me, and a number of new openings and opportunities. I have seen players and staff come, and go; I have had the wonderful opportunity to meet with people in all kinds of different contexts and I hope and pray in some way I have been a blessing to them. It is a privilege to serve Cambridge United Football Club as their chaplain, to offer support, help, a listening ear and advice if appropriate. But most of all, to be there for the people – players, staff, club officials and supporters, and in so doing, to represent Jesus to those that I meet.

This has been my story as chaplain at Cambridge United Football Club during the 2010/11 season. I hope it has been informative and interesting. But more than that, I hope and pray that this story has been about how God has used an ordinary man to be a blessing and help to others – without God none of this would have been possible.

Appendix

Blue Square Bet Premier League: final table 2010/11

		Home			Away						
	Pld	W	D	L	W	D	L	GF	GA	GD	PTS
1 Crawley Town	46	18	3	2	13	9	1	93	30	63	105
2 AFC Wimbledon	46	17	3	3	10	6	7	83	47	36	90
3 Luton Town	46	14	7	2	9	8	6	85	37	48	84
4 Wrexham	46	13	7	3	9	8	6	66	49	17	81
5 Fleetwood Town	46	12	8	3	10	4	9	68	42	26	78
6 Kidderminster	46	13	6	4	7	11	5	74	60	14	72*
7 Darlington	46	13	6	4	5	11	7	61	42	19	71
8 York City	46	14	6	3	5	8	10	55	50	5	71
9 Newport County	46	11	7	5	7	8	8	78	60	18	69
10 Bath City	46	10	10	3	6	5	12	64	68	-4	63
11 Grimsby Town	46	7	12	4	8	5	10	72	62	10	62
12 Rushden & Diamonds	46	10	6	7	6	8	9	65	62	3	62†
13 Mansfield Town	46	9	6	8	8	4	11	73	75	-2	61
14 Kettering Town	46	8	8	7	7	5	11	64	75	-11	58§
15 Gateshead	46	8	9	6	6	6	11	65	68	-3	57
16 Hayes & Yeading	46	10	2	11	5	4	14	57	81	-24	51
17 Cambridge United	46	7	7	9	4	10	9	53	61	-8	50
18 Barrow	46	9	6	8	3	8	12	52	67	-15	50
19 Tamworth	46	6	8	9	6	5	12	62	83	-21	49
20 Forest Green	46	7	10	6	3	6	14	53	72	-19	46
21 Southport	46	9	6	8	2	7	14	56	77	-21	46¶
22 Altrincham	46	6	8	9	5	3	15	47	87	-40	44
23 Eastbourne Borough	46	6	5	12	4	4	15	62	104	-42	39
24 Histon	46	4	3	16	4	6	13	41	90	-49	28**

* Kidderminster Harriers were deducted five points for submitting misleading financial information.
† Rushden & Diamonds were deducted five points for submitting misleading financial information and subsequently expelled from the Football Conference on 11 June 2011.
§ Kettering Town were deducted two points for fielding an ineligible player.
¶ Southport were reprieved from relegation.
**Histon were deducted five points for submitting misleading financial information.

Cambridge United Player Statistics 2010/11

First Team Appearances

	LGE	FAC	FAT	TOTAL
Mark Bentley	6	0	0	6
Luke Berry	12(2)	0	0	12(2)
James Brighton	0(1)	0	0	0(1)
Simon Brown	32	0	0	32
Paul Carden	24	3	3	30
Daryl Clare	10(10)	0(1)	1(1)	11(12)
Darryl Coakley	4(2)	0	1	5(2)
Josh Coulson	36(3)	3	3	42(3)
Jack Eades	0(1)	0	0	0(1)
Wayne Gray	14(9)	3	3	20(9)
Courtney Herbert	0(1)	0	0	0(1)
Blaine Hudson	0(2)	0	0	0(2)
Liam Hughes	10(8)	0	0	10(8)
Sam Ives	4(11)	0	0	4(11)
Shaun Jeffers	0(2)	0	0	0(2)
James Jennings	38	3	2	43
Adam Marriott	10(24)	0	0(3)	10(27)
Rory McAuley	29(7)	3	0	32(7)
Adam Miller	5	0	0	5
Danny Naisbitt	15	3	3	21
David Partridge	27(2)	2	3	32(2)
Jordan Patrick	15(12)	0(1)	1	16(13)
Conal Platt	20(9)	0(1)	0(3)	20(13)
Kevin Roberts	36(1)	3	3	42(1)
Simon Russell	31	3	3	37
Brian Saah	37(2)	1	2	40(2)
Alex Stavrinou	7	0	0	7
Dean Sinclair	6(1)	0	0	6(1)
Jonathon Thorpe	2(3)	0	0	2(3)
Dan Walker	4(2)	0	0	4(2)
Ricky Wellard	9	0	0	9
Robbie Willmott	26(1)	3	3	32(1)
Danny Wright	46	3	2(1)	51(1)

Substitute appearances in brackets.

First Team Scorers

	LGE	FAC	FAT	TOTAL
Danny Wright	10	1	2	13
Robbie Willmott	9	0	0	9
Wayne Gray	7	1	0	8
Simon Russell	6	1	1	8
Brian Saah	3	0	2	5
Josh Coulson	4	0	0	4
Adam Marriott	3	0	1	4
Liam Hughes	2	0	0	2
Jordan Patrick	2	0	0	2
Mark Bentley	1	0	0	1
Luke Berry	1	0	0	1
Daryl Clare	1	0	0	1
James Jennings	1	0	0	1
Dean Sinclair	1	0	0	1
Alex Stavrinou	1	0	0	1
Rory McAuley	0	1	0	1
David Partridge	0	0	1	1
Kevin Roberts	0	0	1	1
Own Goals	1	0	0	1

With thanks to Mark Johnson and the Cambridge United matchday programme.